Gifts From the Ascended Christ

Restoring the Place of the 5-fold Ministry

Robert Stone

DESTINY IMAGE® PUBLISHERS, INC.
P.O. Box 310, Shippensburg, PA 17275-0310
"Promoting Inspired Lives."

This book and all other Destiny Image and Destiny Image Fiction
books are available at Christian bookstores and distributors
worldwide.

For more information on foreign distributors, call 717-532-3040.
Or reach us on the Internet: www.destinyimage.com

ISBN 13 TP: 978-0-7684-1770-8
ISBN 13 EBook: 978-0-7684-1771-5
HC ISBN: 978-0-7684-1773-9
LP ISBN: 978-0-7684-1772-2
Previously Published with ISBN: 1-56043-343-4

For Worldwide Distribution, Printed in the U.S.A.
1 2 3 4 5 6 7 8 9 10 11 / 21 20 19 18 17

Dedication

This book is dedicated to my wonderful wife, Susan. Her dedication to the ways of God continues to both inspire and encourage me to press on in my understanding of God's Kingdom and the Lord Jesus Christ.

Endorsements

"The hallmark of the Christian Church is her ability to articulate her faith and creeds through the written page and the spoken word. Long before the modern Church began her proliferation across the globe, the *ancient* Church of Jesus Christ proclaimed her faith to an unbelieving world through her distinctive pronouncements and writings.

"Bishop Dwayne Stone is one of the best examples of old-fashioned faith with a healthy modern application. His unique messages and treatment of the use of the five-fold ministry in this latter day is a book *every full gospel, pentecostal-apostolic* preacher should have at his or her fingertips. I have made this text a priority for candidates for ordination within my own reformation and I would encourage the brethren of like faiths to offer this volume as an elective among their elder candidates.

"Bishop Stone's vital and godly piety is a beacon on this vast sea of voices, proclaiming the unsearchable riches of His grace."

—J. Delano Ellis, II
Presiding Bishop, United Pentecostal Churches of Christ

"*Gifts From the Ascended Christ: Restoring the Place of the Five-Fold Ministry* is must reading for all who seek revelation of the ministry of Jesus and of God's plans for His Church in the new millennium. It is a line-upon-line, precept-upon-precept teaching of the history, government, and five-fold ministry of the Church. Dwayne Stone presents an excellent and concise explanation of God's plan and purpose for the eldership in the New Testament Church. Every believer should read this book."

—Bishop Carlton D. Pearson
Presiding Bishop, Azusa Interdenominational Fellowship
Senior Pastor, Higher Dimensions Family Church, Tulsa, Oklahoma

"During the 20 years I have known Bishop Stone, it has been obvious that God's touch rested mightily upon him. His latest work, *Gifts From the Ascended Christ,* is a powerful, in-depth study. It is invaluable for those seeking understanding in that it presents a sound biblical basis for the five-fold ministry gifts. Bishop Stone delivers a relevant message that will impact the life of the reader!"

—Robert G. Florence
Pastor, First Assembly of God, Enid, Oklahoma

Contents

Introduction

This book was conceived and given birth to through a series of messages given at Jubilee Faith Center in Denton, Texas. These messages have been an inspiration to many people. I am greatly appreciative to the Holy Spirit for giving me divine illumination and understanding. I am convinced (and I have recently heard other great Christian leaders say the same thing) that the next great move of God will have a "team" mentality. We are coming full circle. The presence and power seen in the Book of Acts is about to burst upon the scene.

In the coming year we are going to hear more about the fivefold ministry of apostles, prophets, evangelists, pastors, and teachers. God is moving in an awesome manner. We must pursue Him. We must seek His face. We must endeavor to grasp His wisdom and revelation.

Everything in the earth realm moves through the process of formation and reformation. The creation of the earth, the creation of man, and even the Old Testament ministry of the tabernacle and temple (which had been completely destroyed by the end of the Babylonian captivity) had to endure God's process. By the time of the birth of Jesus Christ, tradition (a form of godliness) had nullified the word (information) of God. The world needed and received new information (a spoken word), which brought about transformation and the reformation of God's intended initial purpose for man.

In this day God is bringing about reformation in the realm of true apostolic and prophetic ministry. The five-fold ministry of apostles, prophets, evangelists, pastors, and teachers—gifts from the ascended life—is being restored. The ministry of these gifts is being formed and released into new understanding. God's chosen ones are being set in office by the Holy Spirit. The Church is being equipped (informed) and perfected (transformed).

God's people are now realizing that they are forever His redeemed. The Scriptures say that God created Jacob, but formed Israel (see Is. 43:1). As spiritual Israel, we have future deliverance from troubles of any kind. We have the promise of "seed" being gathered to us. No weapon "formed" against us will prosper because Christ is being "formed" in us!

Everything that God forms, He fills. Everything He fills, He finishes. The writer to the Hebrews tells us in chapter 9 verses 12-15 that we are being "filled up" with God's eternal redemption. This redemption establishes us as having an eternal covenant with the Creator of the universe and the Redeemer of mankind. It is through this "new testament" that we receive an eternal inheritance. We are heirs of God and joint-heirs with Jesus Christ.

I am convinced that we are being finished and reformed in preparation for the coming restoration of God in the earth. It is exciting to see the hand of God stretching into its complete purpose.

Chapter One

The Hand of the Lord

Here is the man whose name is the Branch, and He will branch out from His place and build the temple of the Lord (Zechariah 6:12b).

...I will build My church, and the gates of Hades will not overcome it (Matthew 16:18).

Something exciting is happening in the Christian Church today. As we stand poised on the edge of a new millennium, change is in the air. God is doing a mighty work the likes of which we have never seen. Not since the first century has the Church been as close as she now is to fulfilling her holy calling and divine destiny.

For nearly 2000 years the Church has labored to carry out the commission she received from the Lord when He said, "Go into all the world and preach the good news to all creation" (Mk. 16:15b) and "...go and make disciples of all nations, baptizing them in the name of the Father and of

1

the Son and of the Holy Spirit, and teaching them to obey everything I have commanded you" (Mt. 28:19-20a). In all that time the Church's efforts have not surpassed, or even matched, the labor of the earliest generations of believers. Their zeal and success have never been equaled.

Motivated by love for their risen Lord and fortified by the presence of God that descended with power on Pentecost, the Church of the Book of Acts turned their world upside down and all but transformed its culture. By the end of the first century, the gospel had been carried to the farthest regions of the Roman Empire. Beginning at home, these earliest believers were faithful witnesses for Christ "in Jerusalem, and in all Judea and Samaria, and to the ends of the earth" (Acts 1:8b).

Something was lost somewhere along the way, however, because the Church since the first century has generally displayed neither the same evangelistic fervor nor the level of spiritual power evident in the New Testament Church. Not until the twentieth century, and the latter part of the century in particular, has the Church even begun to exhibit in any significant way the qualities of that first generation.

What the Lord is doing today in His Church can only be described as restoration—returning the Church to her original condition as revealed in the Book of Acts. God is accomplishing this by building—or rather, *re*building—His Church according to His own plan, as is clearly laid out in His Word, rather than according to the plans, thoughts, or imaginations of men. Today Jesus is reclaiming His place as the Head of the Church and reasserting His right to mold and equip her to fulfill His purpose.

For this reason and others it is an exciting time to be a Christian. The Lord's plan of restoration involves all of us: everyone who claims the name of Jesus as Savior and Lord.

The Hand of the Lord

His Body, the Church, is not complete until every member is in place, faithfully serving with power, confidence, and freedom.

The Arm of the Lord

The truth that Jesus will build the Church is revealed even in the Old Testament. The prophet Zechariah wrote,

Here is the man whose name is the Branch, and He will branch out from His place and build the temple of the Lord. It is He who will build the temple of the Lord, and He will be clothed with majesty and will sit and rule on His throne. And He will be a priest on His throne. And there will be harmony between the two (Zechariah 6:12b-13).

From our perspective the "Branch" clearly refers to Jesus, who would build the Lord's temple and reign as both Priest and King. Doesn't this passage sound similar to Jesus' own words in Matthew: "...I will build My church, and the gates of Hades will not overcome it" (Mt. 16:18b)?

In a similar manner, the prophet Isaiah wrote, "Who has believed our message and to whom has the arm of the Lord been revealed?" (Is. 53:1) The "arm of the Lord" refers to the Messiah, the "suffering servant" of Isaiah 53. John unmistakably links this reference to Jesus: "Even after Jesus had done all these miraculous signs in their presence, they still would not believe in Him. This was to fulfill the word of Isaiah the prophet: 'Lord, who has believed our message and to whom has the arm of the Lord been revealed?' " (Jn. 12:37-38) Jesus is the "arm of the Lord" through whom all the purposes of God are built up and established.

Any arm that is to be effective and to fulfill its destiny must have a hand connected to it. The hand is used for building. Strength may come from the arm, but the hand does the work. Wouldn't it be very difficult to build something if you had arms but no hands? No matter what the project—birdhouse, doghouse, outhouse, townhouse, or church house—you can't build it without hands.

So if Isaiah 53 tells us that Jesus is the "arm of the Lord," and if Jesus Himself said, "I will build My church," then somewhere along the line there must be a hand by which the building will be done. How then does Jesus build His Church?

Building the Church

Jesus Christ established the Church to be His Body on the earth to bring to completion the work He began of reconciling the world to God (see 2 Cor. 5:18-19). We are to proclaim His death, burial, and resurrection; to teach His Word; to make disciples in His name; and to manifest His life in our lives. To this end Jesus promised, "surely I am with you always, to the very end of the age" (Mt. 28:20b). To this promise of His presence Jesus added the provision of His power: "But you will receive power when the Holy Spirit comes on you; and you will be My witnesses in Jerusalem, and in all Judea and Samaria, and to the ends of the earth" (Acts 1:8). Furthermore, Jesus has provided us with everything we need to grow, mature, and prosper. These "grace gifts," which are granted by the Holy Spirit as He determines, are given so that we can build up and encourage one another. The gifts include: the word of wisdom, the word of knowledge, faith, healing gifts, miraculous powers, prophecy, spiritual discernment, tongues, and interpretation of tongues (see 1 Cor. 12:7-11).

Jesus also gave "ministry gifts" for the specific purpose of building the Church. Paul lists these in the fourth chapter of Ephesians:

4

The Hand of the Lord

It was He [Jesus] *who gave some to be apostles, some to be prophets, some to be evangelists, and some to be pastors and teachers, to prepare God's people for works of service, so that the body of Christ may be built up until we all reach unity in the faith and in the knowledge of the Son of God and become mature, attaining to the whole measure of the fullness of Christ* (Ephesians 4:11-13).

This "five-fold ministry" of apostle, prophet, evangelist, pastor, and teacher should be evident in the life of any church that is fulfilling God's purpose. These ministry gifts are to be active until the Church as a whole reaches maturity, which is "unity in the faith and…[the] knowledge of the Son of God" and attains "the whole measure of the fullness of Christ." Who would argue the fact that the Church has not yet reached this level of unity and maturity? We are still divided in many ways. Likewise, we do not yet see the fullness of Christ manifested in His whole Body. If we are to see this unity and maturity, the five ministry gifts from the ascended Christ must become visible and active in the Church worldwide.

We can think of this five-fold ministry as a five-fingered hand that is connected to Jesus' arm. He uses this "arm of the Lord" to build the Church and to accomplish the Father's purposes. The thumb, forefinger, middle finger, ring finger, and little finger represent the ministry gifts of apostle, prophet, evangelist, pastor, and teacher. Just as a hand functions properly only when all five fingers are intact and healthy, so the Church can fully achieve the Lord's purposes only when all five ministry gifts are present.

The Hand of the Lord

The Old Testament contains numerous references to the "arm" or the "hand" of the Lord. Each instance reveals something about the nature and character of God, with most of them alluding to His power, strength, and will to act. Among other things, the hand of the Lord is a hand of provision: He possesses the power, the strength, and the will to provide for His people. Consider these things that the hand of the Lord provides:

1. ***Power.*** "If the Lord delights in a man's way, He makes his steps firm; though he stumble, he will not fall, for *the Lord upholds him with His hand*" (Ps. 37:23-24). This verse speaks of God's power—that His hand is mighty—which is certainly true. The Word of God tells us that He holds the earth in His hand (see Ps. 95:4). He made all things (see Is. 44:24; 66:1-2a) and "in His hand is the life of every creature and the breath of mankind" (Job 12:10). Truly the Lord's hand is powerful.

2. ***Strength.*** "Then Moses said to the people, 'Commemorate this day, the day you came out of Egypt, out of the land of slavery, because *the Lord brought you out of it with a mighty hand...*' " (Ex. 13:3). In this case "a mighty hand" refers to strength. God delivered Israel from their Egyptian bondage with the strength of His hand.

3. ***Protection.*** "When My glory passes by, I will put you in a cleft in the rock and *cover you with My hand* until I have passed by" (Ex. 33:22). Moses had requested to see God. The Lord answered that no man could see His face and live. However, He agreed to cover Moses with His hand as He passed by and to allow Moses to see His back. The covering hand of God provides protection. As long as we are in the cleft of the rock covered by His hand, we are under His protection. It's not about us getting hold of God but Him getting hold of us.

4. ***Presence.*** "The seventh time the servant reported, '*A cloud as small as a man's hand* is rising from the sea.' So Elijah said, 'Go and tell Ahab, "Hitch up your chariot and go down before the rain stops you" ' " (1 Kings 18:44). After three and a half years of drought, Elijah has seen the fire of God fall on Mount Carmel and has slain the 450 prophets of Baal. Now he is praying for rain and sends out a servant to watch the sky. When the servant returns the seventh time with the report of a cloud the size of a man's hand, Elijah knows that rain is near. In the Old Testament, a cloud often represents more than just rain; many times it represents the presence of God. Whenever we see the *presence* of God in the form of a hand coming toward us, we'd better head for the house because rain is on its way. We are about to see an abundance of God's glory.

   5.   Deliverance. "A thousand may fall at your side, ten thousand at your right hand, but it will not come near you" (Ps. 91:7). Those who trust in the Lord will never be shaken. As with Daniel in the lions' den or Shadrach, Meshach, and Abednego in the fiery furnace, deliverance belongs to those who place their confidence in God.

   6.   Purpose. "Yet, O Lord, You are our Father. We are the clay, You are the potter; we are all the work of Your hand" (Is. 64:8). Our Lord is a God of purpose; He has a reason for everything He does. We are the work—the product—of His hand. The purposeful God created us with purpose. Living in relationship with Him and recognizing Him as our Creator are therefore essential if we are to find and fulfill our purpose.

The "Hand" of the Five-Fold Ministry

   These Scriptures have a direct correlation to the functions and roles of the five-fold ministry. As we study and understand them, we can begin to see why the Lord provided these ministries and offices for the Church. Each one—apostle, prophet, evangelist, pastor, and teacher—was chosen by God and was given to the Church to function within the Body of Christ in a specific way.

The Apostle

The apostle is the "thumb" of the five-fold ministry hand. Not only does it touch the other four but it also provides the gripping or staying power. How much power would our hands have if our thumbs were missing? Not much. Gripping with strength is impossible without the thumb.

In the same way, the apostle's function exemplifies *power*. Wherever you find apostles in the New Testament, you also find power: power to perform signs, wonders, and miracles; power to pull down the strongholds of darkness and hell. Congregations that lack apostolic ministry may have much going on but little being accomplished. This happens because the spiritual power or direction provided by the apostle is missing.

God chose the apostle to govern, that is, to be a bishop set over several congregations for the purpose of establishing the government of the Kingdom of God. Isaiah 9:6 says that the government would be upon the Messiah's shoulders. Jesus has delegated that government to the apostle so that he in turn may govern other believers. The apostle's responsibility is to build a government based not on himself—nor on any human philosophy, thought, or idea—but on the Word of God.

The Prophet

The prophet is the index finger of the five-fold ministry hand. His function involves *purpose* or destiny. Therefore he is always *pointing* at or toward someone or something. When he speaks judgment, the prophet points at us, which is why we sometimes feel uncomfortable around prophets. When addressing purpose, however, the prophet points toward our destiny. Chosen to *exhort* or encourage, the prophet reminds us of who we are, whose we are, where we are going, and what God is doing in our lives. A true prophet's message, although painful at times, will always build up and strengthen; it will *never* tear down or dishearten.

The Evangelist

The evangelist is the middle finger of the five-fold ministry hand. His function is *deliverance* and His purpose is to lead people to salvation in Jesus Christ. In other words, he has been chosen to win the lost to Christ. Just as the middle finger is the center of the hand, so is salvation in Christ the centerpiece of life. Everything else revolves around this. If we do not know Jesus as Savior and Lord, then nothing else makes sense and our lives have no purpose.

The Pastor

The pastor is the ring finger of the ministry hand. Chosen to shepherd the flock of God, the pastor in his function is to provide *protection*. In many respects his responsibility is similar to that of a wedding ring. In a marriage ceremony the wedding band is placed on the fourth finger, which is often called the ring finger. What does the wedding ring signify? It symbolizes the promise to love, honor, cherish, and protect; to become one for life with another. That's the job of the pastor/shepherd as well. He loves, honors, cherishes, and protects the Church, the Bride of Christ, and helps to prepare her for the day when Christ, the great Bridegroom, comes to receive her.

The Teacher

The teacher is the little finger of the five-fold ministry hand. He is chosen to mature the saints, building strength into the Body of Christ, and to bring balance into both the lives of individual believers and the work and ministry of the Church as a whole. Just as the little finger provides overall balance to the human hand, so the teacher balances the other ministry gifts. People who have lost their little finger have to learn to readjust the balance and use of the affected hand. In the same way, teachers help to maintain the proper balance between the apostles, prophets, evangelists, and pastors within the Body of Christ. Without the maturity and balance provided by gifted teachers, the Church as a whole, and individually as local congregations, will not attain the maturity and strength that God intends.

Can you see why all five ministry gifts are important, why we need a full, five-fingered hand to build the Church? We can't function properly or at full potential if even one of these fingers is missing. We need government, but we also need encouragement. We need souls to be won, but we also need shepherds to tend the existing flock. Finally, we need the guidance of wise teachers so that the flock, including both the newborn lambs and the more mature sheep, will grow into a mature, balanced church. When all of the five-fold ministries are present and functioning in harmony, Christ can effectively build His Church.

Qualifying the Ministry Gifts

The Holy Spirit gives gifts as He wills, including the gifts of the five-fold ministry. Before anyone so gifted can effectively use his gifts, however, he must be qualified through a five-step process of separation, suffering, service, being sent, and sonship.

The Hand of the Lord

Separation

The first qualifier in preparation for effective ministry in one of the five-fold functions is *separation*. This means that the person who is being released to function in one of the ministry gifts must be set apart in some way from the rest of the Body. Although all believers, through sanctification, are set apart as God's special people, those Christians called by God to function in one of the five-fold ministries must be further set apart. They cannot effectively operate in their gifts if this does not happen.

A good example of this qualifier is found in the thirteenth chapter of Acts:

> *In the church at Antioch there were prophets and teachers: Barnabas, Simeon called Niger, Lucius of Cyrene, Manaen (who had been brought up with Herod the tetrarch) and Saul. While they were worshiping the Lord and fasting, the Holy Spirit said, "Set apart for Me Barnabas and Saul for the work to which I have called them." So after they had fasted and prayed, they placed their hands on them and sent them off* (Acts 13:1-3).

The church in Antioch, in response to the direction of the Spirit, *set apart* Barnabas and Saul for special work. It was only after they were *separated* out from the rest of the congregation that they could fulfill God's call.

Suffering

The ministry gifts are also qualified through *suffering*. No one likes to embrace, or even talk about, this second qualifier. In fact, it is at this very point of suffering that many people begin to waver, wondering if they have heard and understood God correctly and if He has really called them. All of us have a natural tendency to expect smooth

11

sailing when we are doing God's will. However, the opposite is often the case. Many times our situation becomes more difficult as we follow the Lord in obedience. Usually this is true because we draw the attention and attack of the enemy, a consequence that Jesus warned us would come: "I have told you these things, so that in Me you may have peace. In this world you will have trouble. But take heart! I have over-come the world" (Jn. 16:33).

Jesus' presence with us guarantees that we will overcome the world. Therefore we should see suffering not as some-thing that threatens to destroy us, but as part of the process that prepares us for works of service. In fact, rather than being disheartened when suffering comes our way, we should be encouraged. Paul and Barnabas certainly believed this to be true. After completing their first missionary jour-ney, they revisited Lystra, Iconium, and Antioch, "strength-ening the disciples and encouraging them to remain true to the faith. 'We must go through many hardships to enter the kingdom of God,' they said" (Acts 14:22).

It seems rather amazing that Paul and Barnabas would *encourage* believers by telling them to expect suffering. Yet this is the nature of life in the Kingdom of God (at least while we are on the earth) because the world accepts neither God's Kingdom nor the people who are citizens of His Kingdom. This is why we can expect suffering once we begin to walk in the government of God. We are walking contrary to the ways of sinful man. Yet we can take heart in the knowledge that "...our present sufferings are not worth comparing with the glory that will be revealed in us" (Rom. 8:18).

Service

The third qualifier for the ministry gifts is *service*. Jesus said, "If anyone wants to be first, he must be the very last,

12

and the servant of all" (Mk. 9:35b). Until we learn to be last, we will never be first; until we learn to go to the back, we will never go to the front. If God can't trust us at the back with the little things, He certainly won't entrust us with greater things at the front.

Greatness in the Kingdom of God calls for a servant's heart. Jesus set the example when He washed His disciples' feet and said that He did not come to be served but to serve and to give His life as a ransom for many (see Jn. 13:1-16; Mt. 20:28). It is through faithful, humble service that we become most like Jesus and show God that we possess the kind of heart and spirit that can be trusted with greater things. James 4:10 says, "Humble yourselves before the Lord, and He will lift you up." What position we hold in God's Kingdom has nothing to do with us and everything to do with Him. If we try to climb the ladder ourselves or we push ahead of others to reach first place, we should not be surprised when we don't stay in first place because someone eventually overtakes us.

Why? Self-promotion and promotion by other men include no guarantees. Just as easily as a man promotes another, he can also him bring down. No appointment is secure. When God appoints a man, however, his position is secure because the Lord sustains him. A man appointed by God cannot be brought down by man—or by a denomination—because neither the man nor the denomination lifted him up. God alone is both the qualifier and the sustainer.

Being Sent

The fourth way the five-fold ministry gifts are qualified is through the process of *being sent*. Acts 13:3 says that the church in Antioch, after setting apart Paul and Barnabas, and after a period of prayer and fasting, "placed their hands on them and *sent them off*." Being sent involves a specific commission, an appointed ministry. Those set apart to function in a particular ministry gift are qualified when their ministry or office is recognized and accepted by the Body. The church in Antioch recognized and accepted the ministry to which Paul and Barnabas were called. The outcome of this recognition and acceptance was that the church sent them out to fulfill their calling.

Sonship

The fifth and final qualifier is *sonship*. We are God's children in Christ and through the Holy Spirit. That we are sons and daughters of God is confirmed by the evidence of spiritual gifts in our lives. These gifts are given by the Holy Spirit, and His indwelling presence in each person is God's stamp of ownership. This relationship of *sonship* gives our giftings legitimacy. Apart from Christ and the presence of the Holy Spirit in our lives, both the ministry gifts and the other spiritual gifts given to all God's sons and daughters lack power and purpose.

Growing in the Gifts

Becoming effective in the gifts given by the Holy Spirit is a process of growth that begins with salvation. When we are saved, we are called to serve Christ and the Church. The Holy Spirit equips us with spiritual gifts so that we can fulfill this service. As we recognize and use our gifts, God leads us into ministry within the local body. This is where our gifts are recognized and confirmed by others. After this time of development and training, our gifts then become established as an office, be that of an apostle, a prophet, an evangelist, a pastor, or a teacher.

This maturing of our ministry gifts into an office is always a process. We never receive gifts that are fully grown and completely mature. Instead, through time, energy, and commitment we are required to develop the gifts God gives us. This is part of what Christian growth and maturity are all about. As the gift deposited in us at salvation begins to mature, it gives way to ministry; and ministry, if it develops to maturity, brings the gift all the way into its office.

Many Christians begin to display the Holy Spirit's gift but never persevere until the gifting matures and produces the intended fruit. These believers just are not willing to do all that is necessary to develop their gifting. Sometimes these people go from place to place and church to church never learning who they are or what they're supposed to do. This happens either because they don't understand that growing into their gift is a process or because they are not willing to expend the time and effort to develop their gifting.

Too often believers have a mentality that causes them to expect instant results. We go forward; someone lays hands on us to impart the gifting; we fall on the floor, then get up presuming that we are suddenly going to have a worldwide ministry. It's as though we expect the gifts to be immediately manifested in mature, fully-developed form. How wrong we are! This is not the way God works.

Each one of us has the responsibility to use our gifting until it fulfills the function for which the Spirit gave it. It is up to us to see that our gifting is developed. This occurs through the qualifiers mentioned earlier in this chapter: separation, suffering, service, being sent, and sonship. None of these processes happens overnight. Nor are they matured in us without much effort, time, and practice. Developing and using our ministry gifts requires the same training and learning as acquiring other skills, be they riding a bike, driving a car, or playing basketball. None of these happen by accident.

Many of us are quite willing to stay at our current level of ministry, but the Lord is not satisfied with where we are. He wants to lead us to a higher level. He requires each of us to develop our gifts into ministries, and our ministries into offices.

First Church of the Shriveled Hand

The sixth chapter of Luke records an interesting story from Jesus' three years of ministry on earth:

> *On another Sabbath He went into the synagogue and was teaching, and a man was there whose right hand was shriveled. The Pharisees and the teachers of the law were looking for a reason to accuse Jesus, so they watched Him closely to see if He would heal on the Sabbath. But Jesus knew what they were thinking and said to the man with the shriveled hand, "Get up and stand in front of everyone." So he got up and stood there. Then Jesus said to them, "I ask you, which is lawful on the Sabbath: to do good or to do evil, to save life or to destroy it?" He looked around at them all, and then said to the man, "Stretch out your hand." He did so, and his hand was completely restored. But they were furious and began to discuss with one another what they might do to Jesus* (Luke 6:6-11).

Jesus came into the synagogue one Sabbath and noticed a man with a shriveled hand. This apparently was not a congenital condition. The man's hand had not always been shriveled. At one time or another it had been completely normal, but somewhere along the way something had gone wrong. Some disease had developed until the man's hand had become shriveled, withered, and useless.

The same thing has happened to the Church of Jesus Christ. The "hand" of the five-fold ministry—of the apostle, prophet, evangelist, pastor, and teacher—once functioned correctly, but no longer does. Some disease has devastated the Church so that she no longer impacts the world with the same force as the Church that we see in the Book of Acts.

Somehow, through the course of history, the Church has drifted away from the pure teaching of the Word of God and men have begun to doubt the truth of God's Word. Now the hand of the five-fold ministry is shriveled and the validity of the various spiritual gifts bestowed on the Church by our Lord Jesus Christ is questioned and even denied.

This shriveled state has characterized the five-fold ministry hand for most of the Church's history. Indeed, the manifestation of the gifts in the Church has so declined that the gifts have all but completely disappeared, and those denominations and doctrinal positions that still recognize the ministry gifts embrace only part of the hand. For the most part, the three fingers of the apostle, the prophet, and the evangelist are shriveled up, leaving only the pastor and the teacher to carry on the work of God's Kingdom. This is why the Church, to a great extent, has not fulfilled her mission of taking the gospel of Jesus Christ to the nations and peoples of the world. Her ministry hand is too shriveled to be of much use.

What kind of building is possible with a hand that has only two good fingers? At best, a two-fingered hand may be able to maintain what is already built, but even that will be hard. Yet this is precisely what many, many churches today are doing. They are trying to take care of what the Church has become. They are trying to hang on until the end, when Jesus rescues us from the whole mess. In the meantime there is no building and little growth.

Many of us have grown up in, and even now may be members of, a congregation that could be named the

"First Church of the Shriveled Hand." There is little interest in the concept of the five-fold ministry and even less
understanding of the importance of maintaining a mature,
fully-functioning five-fold hand. Most church members are
basically ignorant of their giftings, and in the rare instance
that they know what their giftings are, they have little avenue
or opportunity to exercise and develop them. To the contrary, tradition is so deeply rooted in most congregations that
it discourages any new concepts or ideas that would challenge
the way things have been done for years. The "First Church
of the Shriveled Hand" needs restoration and healing.

Restoring the Hand

As I mentioned at the beginning of this chapter, the
Lord is in the process of restoring His Church. He is accomplishing this by healing the shriveled hand; by restoring the
five-fold ministry gifts to the Church. Jesus restored the
shriveled hand of the man in the synagogue, whose story is
told in Luke 6:6-11. There is a parallel between this healing
and the healing of the Church that God is initiating today.
Let's look at some of these parallels.

Presenting the Hand

First, Jesus recognized that the man's hand was shriveled
and that something needed to be done. Second, He presented the man's hand to the assembly. In other words, Jesus
called the man up front and made him stand there before
everyone in the synagogue. Third, He raised the man up
and presented him to the whole congregation.

In like manner, the Lord is now bringing the Church's
crippled hand to the attention of His Body. He is showing us
that the hand is indeed shriveled. Ministry has been hindered, the ability to build has been squashed, and the

enemy has kept the hand of God, the five-fold ministry, locked into disease and deficiency and threatened with destruction by the powers of darkness. Some denominations don't want to hear that the five-fold hand of ministry is shriveled. Indeed, many churches refuse to accept that their ministry is hindered, and thousands of preachers don't want to believe that the Church must change how she operates if she wants to fulfill her mandate to introduce the world to Jesus Christ. Nevertheless, God is bringing this to the forefront because He is building His Church, and the gates of hell shall not prevail against her. Whether we want it or not, God is showing us our shriveled hand and telling us that something is definitely lacking in the Church.

One reason for the opposition is that a restoration of the five-fold ministry will force many churches to break with tradition. Jesus was opposed in the synagogue because He healed on the Sabbath day, violating tradition. His ministry totally upset their comfortable routine. Sadly, the same thing is true today. Healing the shriveled hand breaks with tradition as it unleashes the power and glory of God. This has always made "religious" people nervous. If we are among the many Christians who are bound by religion, we are no different from the Pharisees and the teachers of the law who did not want to see Jesus heal the man's hand on the Sabbath.

As God restores the five-fold ministry to the Church in this hour, the Church is faced with a crucial decision. We must choose between God and tradition because the Church as a whole does not want what God is doing. Many believers prefer to sit in the pews singing "Amazing Grace" and waiting for the Lord to return rather than risking an encounter with the power and glory of God. When the Lord heals the five-fold ministry hand, there will be more power, more purpose, and more new lambs born into the fold than the Church has seen for a long time. There will also be a great need for compassionate, caring shepherds who will bring the Body of Christ into maturity. We will have to grow up and become what God wants us to be, and that's a scary thought for many believers.

Stretching the Hand

In Luke 6:10 Jesus told the man with the shriveled hand, "Stretch out your hand." He didn't tell the man to stretch out or hold out his arm; He said, "Stretch out your hand."

How does a man stretch out something that's shriveled? That's certainly bound to hurt! Yet that is precisely what Jesus told the man and what God is telling the Church today. Have you felt this stretching in your life lately? If you want to become effective in exercising your gifts in ministry, you must be prepared for the Lord to stretch you. As long as you are content to stay in your comfort zone, you will never become all that God wants you to be. He wants to raise you up, but first you have to open your hand.

Only God can do the healing work; but He needs your cooperation. He wants you to be obedient to all that He asks of you. That kind of obedience stretches you; it stretches your shriveled hand.

God's plan is to do His work in the earth through us. Paul wrote to the Corinthians, "For the weapons of our warfare are not carnal, but mighty through God to the pulling down of strong holds" (2 Cor. 10:4 KJV). If we are "pulling down" strongholds, we have to be underneath them. Colossians chapter 1 tells us that the Son of God is above everything. So it isn't Jesus who will pull down the strongholds of tradition that bind us, it's us. We must pull down strongholds in Jesus' power and by His authority.

The Hand of the Lord

That's why the shriveled hand of the Church must be restored. It's hard to pull something with a shriveled hand. There's no strength or gripping power. A healthy hand, however, is well-designed both for pulling down and for building up.

For far too long the Church has tried to stand up to the powers of darkness and to pull down strongholds with a shriveled hand. That's why we have known both limited success and little opposition. The enemy has no reason to fear a weakened and debilitated Church. Today, however, the devil is sitting up and taking notice. He fears the restoration of the five-fold ministry because he knows that with the hand fully restored, the Church can reach up into the heavenlies and in the name and authority of Christ pull down demonic strongholds.

God wants to develop in us the apostolic, prophetic, evangelistic, pastoral, and teaching gifts. These gifts give us knowledge and understanding, but if we do not allow them to grow and mature into ministry, and if those ministries do not grow into their offices, we will never do much with them against the powers of darkness.

All that is changing, however. God is getting us ready to use our gifts. He's moving us from our gifting into our ministry so that we may step into our office and cast down imaginations, bringing everything into captivity unto the law of Jesus Christ (see 2 Cor. 10:4-5 KJV).

Restoring the Hand

As the Lord restores this five-fold ministry He is stretching us; He's taking us places we've never been before. In essence, He's restoring the Church to her intended function and purpose. Luke 6:10 says that as the man stretched out

21

his shriveled hand at Jesus' command, his hand was "completely restored."

What does the word "restore" mean except to return something to its original condition? Christ is restoring His Church to her original condition as patterned in the Book of Acts. What was the original condition of the Church? Luke describes it this way:

> *They devoted themselves to the apostles' teaching and to the fellowship, to the breaking of bread and to prayer. Everyone was filled with awe, and many wonders and miraculous signs were done by the apostles. All the believers were together and had everything in common. Selling their possessions and goods, they gave to anyone as he had need. Every day they continued to meet together in the temple courts. They broke bread in their homes and ate together with glad and sincere hearts, praising God and enjoying the favor of all the people. And the Lord added to their number daily those who were being saved* (Acts 2:42-47).

The apostles and other believers in the early Church *reached out with their hands* and healed people, raised up people, and restored people to fellowship with God. In Acts 3:1-8 Peter healed a lame man by *reaching out his hand* and raising the man to his feet. Acts 19:11-12 tells us that God did special miracles "by the hands of Paul" (KJV) in that handkerchiefs and aprons he had touched cured sick people who came into contact with them.

As we use our hands in faith, the hand is restored. This means that the office of the apostle is restored, bringing true government; the office of the prophet is restored, bringing true purpose and destiny; the office of the evangelist is restored, bringing new souls continually into the Kingdom; the office of the pastor is restored, bringing true protection and care for the sheep; and the office of the teacher is restored, bringing new and better understanding of the revelation of God. Through all this, God's people are becoming strong. They are growing up and coming into full maturity.

Because the Lord is restoring the five-fold ministry to His Church, there is no better time than right now to gain a thorough understanding of the distinctiveness and function of each of the offices of these ministry gifts. No matter who you are, where you serve in your church, or what ministry or function you may be involved in, you must understand the place and role of the five-fold ministry if you are to fulfill your function and purpose in your local congregation. Whether you are an elder or a deacon, a teacher or a pastor, the leader of a home group or a believer who is simply trying to understand and fulfill your place and calling in the Body of Christ, there may be elements of one or more of the five-fold ministry gifts operating in your life. Learn to recognize these so that the Lord can use you to build the Church. Do all in your power to be sure that the gifts God has given you grow to their fullest development and effectiveness.

I believe that we who are part of the Church today are living in the most exciting days since the first century! Jesus Christ is restoring His Church. He's preparing you and me to bring in the greatest spiritual harvest in history.

Are you ready? If not, today is the day to start preparing yourself so that God can use you to build the Church. Don't be part of the shriveled hand. Let the Lord work maturity in you. Let Him build His gifts in you as you fulfill your function in His glorious Church, a restored Body that is strong enough to pull down the strongholds of the enemy!

Chapter Two

The Office of the Apostle

And in the church God has appointed first of all apostles...(1 Corinthians 12:28).

Consequently, you are no longer foreigners and aliens, but fellow citizens with God's people and members of God's household, built on the foundation of the apostles and prophets, with Christ Jesus Himself as the chief cornerstone (Ephesians 2:19-20).

The things that mark an apostle—signs, wonders and miracles—were done among you with great perseverance (2 Corinthians 12:12).

I know from first-hand experience some of the problems that can occur when the five-fold ministry is in a withered condition because these gifts from the ascended Christ are not functioning properly. I grew up in a denomination that recognized evangelists, pastors, and teachers but not apostles or prophets. Like most denominations, mine believed that the offices of the apostle and the prophet ceased at the end of the first century. So when I was trying to work out God's call on my life, it was only natural that pastors in my denomination applied pressure on me to conform me to their way of thinking and their way of doing things. The problem was that I had an apostolic gifting, not a pastoral gifting—even though I did not know it at the time. Ignorant of the apostolic office, I tried to conform to the pastoral "mold"; I really did.

This didn't work. My apostolic bent for government and order often clashed with their pastoral bent for care and shepherding. There were times as we met together that some pastors would get out of order and I wanted to stand up and tell them, "You're out of order." They would discuss doctrine, and I wanted to say, "The doctrine is out of order." Or they discussed church government, and I wanted to tell them, "The government you're discussing is out of order." Sometimes when we were in a discussion, they would quote the "rule book" to me and I would turn around and quote God's Word to them. This made them quite angry, and eventually I got a reputation as a rebellious troublemaker. I wasn't rebellious; I simply had a different gifting from theirs.

I did not really begin to grow into my apostolic ministry and office until I got into an apostolic church where the people recognized my apostolic gifting, accepted it and me, and helped me recognize my gifting and develop it. For the first time I wasn't accused of being rebellious. Nor was I told that I was crazy. That congregation provided an environment in which I could grow. From time to time different apostles visited the church. Many singled me out, called me forward, prophesied over me, and laid hands on me. I did not seek them out; they called me out. Gradually I came to realize that God was ordaining my ministry. He was bringing me into an understanding of the apostolic office.

This didn't happen overnight. I went through many struggles. Both my family and my church suffered as I learned to function correctly in the gifting and ministry God had given me. Part of the problem was that I had no example to follow. I had never seen an apostle up close who was functioning in his office. It was not part of my background. I made many mistakes, but gradually, by the grace of God, I learned and grew. Through it all I discovered another truth as well. If the apostle is not functioning in his office, it is impossible for the prophet, the evangelist, the pastor, and the teacher to function properly in their offices.

Recognizing the Apostle

It is impossible to hold the office of apostle without an apostolic gifting and a recognized ministry. In the denomination I grew up in, I was unable to develop and function in my apostolic gifting because it was not a recognized office. Only later, when I went to a church that acknowledged the apostolic office, was I released to grow and develop in that ministry.

In order to have a valid ministry as an apostle, recognition must come from two quarters. First, those who are submitted to the authority of the gift must recognize it in you. In other words, those whom you would seek to lead must recognize the gift in you. Second, those who are already recognized and functioning as apostles must recognize the gifting in you. What this means is that if you think you are an apostle but no one recognizes you as one, then you are not an apostle. If no one else sees the gifting you think you have, then it is not there. A genuine gifting will make itself known.

A Spirit-imparted ministry will reveal itself. Someone will perceive it.

As I said before, few denominations today recognize the office of apostle. Most of them believe that it ended in the first century. Although apostolic people may be recognized today for having great gifts or a powerful ministry, the office God has given them is the true office of bishop. An apostle/bishop is an overseer of churches, elders, ministers, and ministries.

Tracklaying

One day the Lord gave me an illustration to help explain the office of an apostle and how it relates to the rest of the five-fold ministry. In the nineteenth century when railroad companies planned to expand their lines out West, the first thing they did was to send explorers or surveyors to check out the lay of the land and to map out the best route for the railroad to take. Then the company would come in and build the railroad according to the guidelines set out by the surveyors.

The apostle is like the railroad surveyor. He is out front, on the cutting edge. The apostle is the one who goes on ahead, checks out the territory, then comes back and says to the church, "This is where we are going." The ministry of the apostle determines the course for the church. The office of the apostle actually lays the track. Charting the course is no good if you don't provide the means for others to get there. A train will go nowhere without tracks to run on.

So apostles in their office are tracklayers. By the same analogy, then, prophets are the engine crew: the engineer, who keeps the train on the right track; and the fireman, who keeps stoking the engine, who keeps the fire burning so the train has the power to move down the track. The evangelist is the conductor, who gets off at every stop, invites new passengers onto the train, and calls out "All aboard!" The pastor is the porter or steward, who cares for the needs and comfort of the passengers on the train; and the teacher is the tour guide, who explains the sights and sounds along the way, helping the passengers to get ready for their destination. All this is possible only if the tracklayers have done their job.

If no track has been laid, the train will not go anywhere, and if the train's not going anywhere, what's the use of getting on board? If a local congregation, or a denomination or fellowship of churches, doesn't know where it is going, then it is going nowhere. Then the only way to convince people to "get on board" is to provide an attractive building that has padded pews, to hire an impressive preacher, or to have good fellowship or delicious pot-luck dinners. These churches may not be going anywhere, but they'll have fun getting there.

Unfortunately, this describes many churches that do not recognize the office of the apostle. They are going nowhere. Their train is stuck at the station because they either have no track or don't know which track to be on.

Churches that are going somewhere, on the other hand, don't have to depend on external appearances. Store-front buildings, a temporary location, less than first class facilities; these don't matter much if the church is on the move and knows where it is going. People are attracted to such churches because they have purpose and a clear vision; they know where they are going. That's what the apostle is for.

Qualifications for the Office of Apostle/Bishop

What qualifies a person as an apostle? Surely, the recognized gifting is the primary thing. However, not all of us grow into the fullness of the ministry that God intends for us to have. How much we grow depends on how far we are willing to go with Him in order to enter into His purpose. Thus, not everyone with an apostolic gifting will carry through to the fullness of God's plans for them. Those who do will grow to display certain specific qualities. We will look at seven of these characteristics.

1. *Spiritual wisdom.* The church at Corinth was divided over the issue of apostolic authority; not whether to recognize it but *whose* authority to recognize. One of the reasons Paul wrote his first Letter to the Corinthians was to resolve this issue. He gets right to the point in chapter 1 when he appeals to them to "agree with one another so that there may be no divisions among you..." (1 Cor. 1:10b). Some were claiming to follow Paul, others Apollos, others Peter, and still others Christ, all of whom were recognized as apostles by the early Church. This disagreement prompts Paul to ask the pointed question, "Is Christ divided?" (verse 13a). He then describes his apostolic calling: "For Christ did not send me to baptize, but to preach the gospel—not with words of human wisdom, lest the cross of Christ be emptied of its power" (verse 17).

If Paul's message was not based on human wisdom, what was it based on? Very simply, it was based on Christ Himself. Paul wrote, "but we preach Christ crucified: a stumbling block to Jews and foolishness to Gentiles, but to those whom God has called, both Jews and Greeks, Christ the power of God and the wisdom of God" (verses 23-24). After telling the Corinthians that God deliberately chose "the foolish things of the world to shame the wise" and "the weak things of the world to shame the strong" (verse 27), he says, "It is because of Him [God] that you are in Christ Jesus, who has become for us wisdom from God—that is, our righteousness, holiness and redemption" (verse 30).

The Office of the Apostle

Paul's calling and message as an apostle were based on the wisdom from God of "Christ crucified" (verse 23), a message of foolishness in the eyes of the world, but the power of God for everyone who was being saved (see verse 18).

So the first qualification for an apostle is *spiritual wisdom.* Paul describes this wisdom in more detail a few verses later:

> *We do, however, speak a message of wisdom among the mature, but not the wisdom of this age or of the rulers of this age, who are coming to nothing. No, we speak of God's secret wisdom, a wisdom that has been hidden and that God destined for our glory before time began.... We have not received the spirit of the world but the Spirit who is from God, that we may understand what God has freely given us. This is what we speak, not in words taught us by human wisdom but in words taught by the Spirit, expressing spiritual truths in spiritual words* (1 Corinthians 2:6-7,12-13).

The spiritual wisdom of the apostle is not the wisdom of the world, or of the world's leaders, but a wisdom revealed only by the Holy Spirit. It is a wisdom otherwise unknowable by men. This spiritual wisdom enables an apostle to express spiritual truths in spiritual words. The Greek word for "spiritual" in verse 13 is *pneumatikos,* from which we get the word "pneumatic." *Pneumatikos* also means "non-carnal, divinely supernatural, and regenerate."[1]

All of us are familiar with the word "charismatic"; it refers to "gift people," those who believe, understand, and walk in the flow of spiritual gifts. "Pneumatic" is a less familiar word to apply to believers. It refers to "spirit people"—apostles and prophets specifically—who have the ability to function

---

1. James Strong, *Strong's Exhaustive Concordance of the Bible* (Peabody, Massachusetts: Hendrickson Publishers, n.d.), *pneumatikos,* (G#4152).

not only in the realm of the flesh but in the realm of the Spirit also.

A pneumatic is an individual whom God has especially chosen to have supernatural wisdom or a supernatural gifting for the purpose of establishing the foundation of the ministry. This wisdom is not something that can be learned. It doesn't simply land on an individual. Indeed, this kind of spiritual wisdom cannot even be understood in the realm of the flesh. It has to be understood in the realm of the spirit.

2.   Faithfulness. The second qualification for the office of apostle/bishop is faithfulness. Paul wrote, "Now it is required that those who have been given a trust must prove faithful" (1 Cor. 4:2). Jesus said to His disciples,

> *Who then is the faithful and wise servant, whom the master has put in charge of the servants in his household to give them their food at the proper time? It will be good for that servant whose master finds him doing so when he returns. I tell you the truth, he will put him in charge of all his possessions* (Matthew 24:45-47).

Anyone who desires to function in the office of apostle (or any other office) must first be faithful and be *seen* as faithful by others.

Faithfulness cannot be established in three weeks, in three months, or even in three years. *Faithfulness takes time.* There is no short cut. *Faithfulness takes discipline.* There is no quick and easy formula. *Faithfulness takes consistency.* It means being steady and dependable all the time; being trustworthy day in and day out during good times and bad. It means being true to your word, true to your walk, and true to your call, no matter what.

If you want to function in the office of apostle/bishop (or anywhere else), you can't be up one week and down the next, or in church one year and out the next. If you want people to invest in you, you've got to be faithful. There is no substitute for faithfulness. It is absolutely essential.

3. Self-denial. The office of the apostle/bishop also calls for self-denial. According to Jesus, self-denial is a basic requirement of discipleship. "If anyone would come after Me, he must deny himself and take up his cross daily and follow Me" (Lk. 9:23b). In his second Letter to Timothy, Paul wrote, "For God did not give us a spirit of timidity, but a spirit of power, of love and of self-discipline" (2 Tim. 1:7).

Self-discipline is impossible without some degree of self-denial. This does not mean denying ourselves only those things that are evil or are bad for our spiritual or physical health. Sometimes self-denial means saying no to some good things simply because they are not the best that God has for us; they are not worthy of our attention because they may distract us from God's purpose for our lives. There may be nothing wrong with these things, yet they are not part of what God wants for us.

In the ninth chapter of First Corinthians Paul discusses the self-denial he endured for the sake of the gospel, alluding to at least four specific areas. The first of these is self-denial with regard to money. Although Paul vigorously defends his right to earn a living from the gospel (see 1 Cor. 9:1-14), he also says that he deliberately chose not to avail himself of that right. "If others have this right of support from you, shouldn't we have it all the more? But we did not use this right. On the contrary, we put up with anything rather than hinder the gospel of Christ" (1 Cor. 9:12). Rather than earn his living from the gospel, Paul supported himself as a tent maker (see Acts 18:2-3).

Paul also mentioned self-denial in the area of service. He saw himself as a bond servant of Christ and a servant of the gospel to all men. "Though I am free and belong to no man, I make myself a slave to everyone, to win as many as possible" (1 Cor. 9:19). Paul did not flaunt his "status" as an apostle. To the contrary, he was always amazed that he, the "chief of sinners" (see 1 Tim. 1:15 KJV), was even a recipient of God's grace. Paul did not put himself on a pedestal. Nor was he afraid of hard work. He put his shoulder to the task to do whatever was necessary to get the job done. Apostles must be willing to serve rather than insist on *being served.* That takes self-denial.

An apostle also has to practice self-denial through flexibility—being able to adapt to changing times, circumstances, and situations. Paul told the Corinthians that he adapted himself to fit the people he was trying to win (see 1 Cor. 9:20-22). He did this not by compromise, but by seeking common points of reference with his audience. His goal was to win souls to the Kingdom of God. "I have become all things to all men so that by all possible means I might save some" (1 Cor. 9:22b). Paul's flexibility extended to his personal circumstances as well. He wrote to the Philippians, "I have learned to be content whatever the circumstances....I have learned the secret of being content in any and every situation, whether well fed or hungry, whether living in plenty or in want" (Phil. 4:11b-12). Paul was confident that God was in control of his life. Any circumstance, any sacrifice, was acceptable as long as he was in God's will.

Finally, self-denial means putting the body (the flesh with its lusts and desires) under complete subjection. Paul wrote,

> *Do you not know that in a race all the runners run, but only one gets the prize? Run in such a way as to get the prize....Therefore I do not run like a man running aimlessly; I do not fight like a man beating the air. No, I beat my body and make it my slave so that after I have preached to*

The Office of the Apostle

others, I myself will not be disqualified for the prize
(1 Corinthians 9:24,26-27).

Paul exercised self-control regarding his own desires in order to remain true to his calling. Subjection of the body also has to do with a willingness to fast when called for; an awareness that the strength of the body comes not from the dinner table but from the Lord.

4. *Embrace suffering.* This is the qualification that no one likes to talk about. We would all be happier if the Bible didn't speak of suffering as part of the life of a believer. However, Jesus warned us that we would face tribulation in the world. Suffering is inescapable. It is part of being a member of the human family, and even more a part of being a member of God's family. An apostle is well aware of this and has learned not only to endure suffering but to embrace it. He understands that in order to minister effectively to everyone whom God brings across his path, he must accept the fact that suffering on his part may be necessary in order to help bring forth God's perfect work in the hearts of others. For an apostle, suffering is an "occupational hazard" of doing the Lord's work. Paul wrote about this in Second Corinthians 6:3-10 where he talks about troubles, hardships, distresses, beatings, imprisonments, sleepless nights, hunger, and other difficulties...all endured for the sake of the gospel.

One thing that suffering does is to help us learn obedience. In this, as in everything else, Jesus Christ Himself is our example. Speaking of Jesus, the writer of Hebrews said, "Although He was a son, He learned obedience from what He suffered and, once made perfect, He became the source of eternal salvation for all who obey Him" (Heb. 5:8-9). If

Jesus learned obedience through suffering, how much more then should we!

5. ***The desire and ability to build the Body of Christ and bring it to maturity.*** An apostle has a heart for the Body of Christ, the Church; a longing and a burning desire to see believers and churches built up in Christ and firmly established in the faith. Paul's letters provide a good illustration of this because in them he openly reveals his heart for the people of God.

> *First, I thank my God through Jesus Christ for all of you...God...is my witness how constantly I remember you in my prayers at all times...I long to see you so that I may impart to you some spiritual gift to make you strong* (Romans 1:8-11).

> *My dear children, for whom I am again in the pains of childbirth until Christ is formed in you* (Galatians 4:19).

> *I have not stopped giving thanks for you, remembering you in my prayers. I keep asking that the God of our Lord Jesus Christ, the glorious Father, may give you the Spirit of wisdom and revelation, so that you may know Him better* (Ephesians 1:16-17).

> *God can testify how I long for all of you with the affection of Christ Jesus* (Philippians 1:8).

In addition to a heart for the Body of Christ, an apostle has the Spirit-given ability to build the Church and bring it to maturity. As I mentioned earlier, an apostle can communicate spiritual truths with spiritual words. The work of an apostle is also accompanied by signs and wonders that serve to build and establish the Church.

6. ***An individual who is completely sold out to God and His purposes.*** An apostle must have an undivided heart that is

The Office of the Apostle

focused entirely on God. There must be no greater priority, no higher love, no deeper commitment than to the Person, the purposes, and the will of God. King David of Israel was called "a man after His [God's] own heart" (1 Sam. 13:14). So should an apostle be. Paul said, "For to me, to live is Christ and to die is gain" (Phil. 1:21), and "I have been crucified with Christ and I no longer live, but Christ lives in me. The life I live in the body, I live by faith in the Son of God, who loved me and gave Himself for me" (Gal. 2:20).

7. *A public ministry.* A public ministry is out in the open for everyone to see. The apostle's ministry should be a recognized ministry characterized by seven specific elements:

1. *Faith.* This means learning to live and walk by faith; being willing to step out where other people aren't willing to go. Faith provides the vision for the apostle to scout ahead, chart the course, and lay the track for the rest to follow.

2. *Signs and wonders.* Tracklayers encounter all kinds of obstacles. Sometimes mountains get in the way. Then either a tunnel must be built through the mountain or the mountain must be removed. Signs and wonders are for the moving of mountains.

3. *Giving.* The apostle must show his willingness to give of his finances, of his time, of his energy, of everything that he is and has. If he is not ready to give whatever is necessary to lay the track, how can he expect that others will give to complete the course he has charted?

4. *Prophetic preaching.* Prophetic preaching establishes a destination. It passes on the vision of where the church is supposed to go. If you don't know where you are going, then any track will do. Prophetic

preaching identifies the correct track so that the congregation arrives at the desired destination.

5. *Doctrinal teaching.* Tracks must have a solid foundation under them. Otherwise they will sink and shift, the train will derail, and disaster will follow. The vision and path the church is to follow must have a solid underpinning of scriptural truth and teaching.

6. *Leadership.* If an apostle lays track but no one follows him, what has he accomplished? He must inspire confidence, effectively communicate the vision, and exercise wise leadership if the church is to follow him along the course he has charted.

7. *Sensitivity to the Spirit.* Without spiritual sensitivity the apostle would not know where to go, what to do, or how to do it. Neither would he be able to catch God's vision or pass it on to those who follow him. The church would then be hindered from discovering and fulfilling God's purpose.

The Function of the Office of Apostle/Bishop

There are seven functions to the office of apostle/bishop.

1. Plant churches that are relevant to the times and the society. An apostle has the desire to plant churches that are relevant; that speak to people today where they live, in a language they can understand. Many churches have lost touch with where people are and what they need. Because of habit or tradition or deadness, their worship, their music, and their teaching have lost meaning for themselves as well as for the people outside the church doors. It's no surprise that these congregations reach few people for Christ and have little impact on the culture.

The Office of the Apostle

A church that wants to reach people must relate to its society and culture in a relevant way. There must be something there that both addresses current needs and looks toward the future. Such a church must be willing to regularly reevaluate where it is and what it is doing; adapting, modifying, and changing its methods and ministries (but *not* its message) as necessary to remain relevant. The apostle/bishop seeks to establish a beachhead for the future and to look to what God wants to do tomorrow, next week, next year, and 50 years from now.

So how do you plant a relevant church? There are several important points to consider.

1. *Impart faith.* There's a difference between *preaching* faith and *imparting* faith. It's not necessary to be in the pulpit to impart faith. If you have the ability to impart, you can do it anywhere: at a restaurant, at a home fellowship, at home, one-on-one. I don't necessarily have to *preach* every word God gives me. Sometimes it is more effective when I share it one-on-one with another person simply because that's when God is imparting through my life.

2. *Lay a proper foundation.* Jesus said that a house built on the sand would collapse when the rains came (see Mt. 7:26-27). Only a house built on a solid foundation of rock will stand through the storm. This proper and secure foundation can be only one thing. It's not the personality of the preacher, the character of the bishop, or the gifting of the elders. The *only* sure foundation for a church is the Word of God. Jesus said, "Heaven and earth will pass away, but My words will never pass away" (Mt. 24:35). Nothing built of man will last. Only God's Word will stand.

3. *Penetrate new territory.* This means blazing a trail both geographically and spiritually; entering areas where the gospel has not gone before and engaging the enemy in his own camp. It's like the popular revival song that says, "I went into the enemy's camp and took back what he stole from me."

4. *Inspire the dynamics of an apostolic church.* As an overseer, an apostle/bishop should inspire a church, or a group of churches, to grow and display the dynamics and characteristics of an apostolic church. What is an apostolic church? The best example we have is the Church in the Book of Acts, where we can find seven particular distinctives of an apostolic church:

   • *Influences the city through each one's "personal ministry."* The Church in the Book of Acts turned its world upside down with the gospel. An apostolic church is actively engaged in ministries, programs, and outreach to influence its entire city and region for Christ. It doesn't "circle the wagons"; it goes on the offensive.

   • *Recognizes and acknowledges the importance of the ministries of women.* Women played an important role in the ministry of the New Testament Church. Nowhere in the New Testament does Paul or any other apostle deny the active involvement of women in ministry. In fact, in every town Paul visited, God raised up women to help him in his work. He made no distinction between Aquila and Priscilla, and in Galatians 3:28 said that in Christ there is neither male nor female. The much-quoted First Corinthians 14:34-35 is probably best understood within the cultural environment of the day as an injunction against disruptive speech during worship, rather than as an out-and-out prohibition of women speaking in church. An apostolic church openly receives the Spirit-led ministry of women.

- *Maintains a positive outlook in the midst of resistance.* Every time the New Testament Church suffered (which was often) they sang. Whenever trouble came, they didn't moan and groan; they prayed and sang until God's power was manifested and the chains fell off or the doors flew open. They worshiped until the victory was won. No matter what's going on in your life, if you can't be positive, focusing on the Lord, something is wrong. By keeping its eyes on Jesus an apostolic church remains positive even in negative circumstances.

- *Establishes order and experiences spontaneity—together.* Order in the church helps ensure that everyone remains on the right track, headed in the right direction. Spontaneity helps inject life and excitement into the journey. Both are important. Order alone leads to boredom, empty tradition, and meaningless ritual; spontaneity alone, on the other hand, eventually results in chaos and scriptural and doctrinal error. The two together produce balance and an environment for dynamic growth.

- *Builds on the Word of God—not the gift.* It's easy to build a church around someone's gift. The only problem is that the church collapses if the person with the gift leaves or the gift falls apart. A church built on the Word of God will remain because the

Word of God stands forever.

- *Is structured for long-term growth and effectiveness.* Many churches today have built their track into a circle and are going nowhere—same sermons, same songs, same structure, same everything— while the world around them continues to change. They are like Israel in the wilderness, going around and around the same mountain and never getting anywhere. That generation of Israel ultimately died in the wilderness. An apostolic church looks to the future and moves ahead with confidence to enter the promised land of God's purpose of reaching the nations.

- *Is positive and creative in its approach to ministry.* An apostolic church is always looking for new methods, timely ministries, and creative strategies to make the never-changing message of Christ continually relevant in an ever-changing society and culture.

2.   *Oversee and strengthen churches and ministers.* In the fourteenth chapter of Acts Luke says of Paul and Barnabas:

They preached the good news in that city [Derbe] *and won a large number of disciples. Then they returned to Lystra, Iconium and Antioch, strengthening the disciples and encouraging them to remain true to the faith. "We must go through many hardships to enter the kingdom of God," they said. Paul and Barnabas appointed elders for them in each church and, with prayer and fasting, committed them to the Lord, in whom they had put their trust* (Acts 14:21-23).

In these verses we see Paul and Barnabas performing the apostolic functions of oversight and strengthening. On the return leg of their first missionary journey, the two apostles revisited churches they had established earlier and encouraged the believers, strengthening them and establishing them firmly in the faith by additional preaching and teaching. Apparently the churches had grown and matured to the point where gifted leaders had risen up and were ready to take on the responsibilities of eldership. Paul and Barnabas recognized the gifting of these leaders and validated their ministries before the churches by appointing them as elders. These new elders would then give consistent, healthy, long-term leadership to the churches.

The apostle/bishop has the responsibility to provide oversight and guidance to the churches and individuals under his care and to strengthen, encourage, and affirm the giftings and ministries of growing leaders whom the Lord is raising up.

3. Develop new leaders. Apostles in the New Testament were always alert to identify believers in the churches who were gifted and called as leaders. Part of their function was to train these leaders and then to release them into their ministries. This is seen most clearly in the earthly ministry of Jesus Christ Himself, the chief apostle, when He chose His disciples. These twelve men, called out from a larger body of followers, were brought into a more intimate circle with Jesus where He taught them, developed them, and trained them to do the work of apostles. Paul and Barnabas, as we have already seen, also followed this pattern. They recognized and appointed new leaders as elders in the churches under their care. An apostle/bishop has the ability and the responsibility to identify, recognize, call out, raise up, train, develop, encourage, and appoint new leadership in the churches under his care.

4.   Ordain ministries. Apostles have been given the authority and responsibility to ordain three types of ministry:

1. *Elders,* which in the New Testament included other apostles, prophets, evangelists, pastors, and teachers.
2. *Ministers.*
3. *Deacons.*

The apostolic gift is no greater or more important than any of the other gifts; it is simply *first* in order. First Corinthians 12:28 says, "And in the church God has appointed *first of all* apostles...." It is a priority of order, not of importance. All the ministry gifts are equally important. The apostolic office could not function without the other four. What good is a hand that has a thumb but no fingers?

The order is apostles, then prophets, then evangelists, then pastors, and finally teachers. This is also the direction that ordination flows. An apostle can ordain all the others, but can himself be ordained only by another apostle. Ordination flowing in the other direction is out of order. In other words, a teacher cannot ordain a pastor, a pastor cannot ordain an evangelist, etc. By priority of position and order, the apostle/bishop has the responsibility for ordaining the other ministries.

5.   Supervise and coordinate ministries. What this basically means is that an apostle/bishop has the responsibility to fix problems, fill positions, and provide accountability. A large part of Paul's first Letter to the Corinthians was devoted to answering questions they had regarding various aspects of belief and practice. Paul also gave considerable attention to correcting abuses related to the observance of the Lord's Supper and the exercising of spiritual gifts. All of these were problems that needed to be addressed. The early churches also needed regular, local leadership. Apostles like Paul and

The Office of the Apostle

Barnabas, as we saw earlier, appointed elders to fill these needs. As far as accountability was concerned, Paul and the other apostles represented to the churches the power and authority of Christ Himself. They also had the authority to call others in the churches to account for their leadership and actions. A good example of this is in Acts chapter 5 when Peter pronounces judgment on Ananias and Sapphira for lying to the Holy Spirit.

6.   *Manage crisis.* Every now and then crises arise in the church that if not properly managed can destroy the church and the ministries of the leaders. In situations such as this, the buck stops with the apostle/bishop. Crisis management is part of his function. Two examples from the early Church come to mind. The first is in Acts chapter 6 when dissension over the distribution of food to the poor in the church in Jerusalem threatened the unity and harmony of the fellowship. Peter and the other disciples got together and directed the congregation to choose six men from the local body to deal with the problem. The result gave birth to the ministry of deacons. The second situation is found in the fifteenth chapter of Acts, where the question of whether or not Gentile believers should be required to be circumcised and to obey other aspects of the Jewish law is addressed. The church in Jerusalem convened a council, which Paul and Barnabas attended from Antioch, to resolve the issue. The apostolic leadership determined that no additional requirements should be made of Gentile Christians other than to abstain from eating meat that had been sacrificed to idols and from sexual immorality. The decision was a great victory for the principle of spiritual liberty in Christ.

7.   *Network with other ministries.* The apostle/bishop seeks to network with other ministries because he under-

stands that strength comes through cooperation and unity. In Romans 15:25-27 and First Corinthians 16:1-4 Paul refers to a collection of money from the churches of Asia for the relief of the beleaguered church in Jerusalem. He networked and coordinated with these churches so that the collection would go smoothly. An apostle/bishop is in a perfect position to serve as a liaison between different churches and ministries to help coordinate and strengthen overall efforts to advance the gospel.

The apostle/bishop is the first in order of the offices of the five-fold ministry. His office provides government, order, stability, and guidance. He is the tracklayer. Second in line of order is the prophet. He provides the fire that moves the train (the church) down the track. Both the track and the fire are needed for a balanced church. The apostle shows us where to go; the prophet shows us how to get there.

Chapter Three

The Office of the Prophet

When a prophet of the Lord is among you, I reveal Myself to him in visions, I speak to him in dreams (Numbers 12:6b).

Do not touch My anointed ones; do My prophets no harm (Psalm 105:15).

Ministerial burnout has reached epidemic proportions in our day. Every month hundreds of pastors and other clergy of all denominations and fellowships resign or are forced out of their positions, many of them leaving the professional ministry altogether. There are many reasons for this, but I believe that one of the most significant is unreasonable expectations. In most churches and denominations the pastor or senior pastor is expected to function in every role—prophet, priest, and king. He is looked to for organizational, relational, and spiritual leadership in equal amounts of time, effort, and quality. The church expects him to be apos-

47

tle, prophet, evangelist, pastor, and teacher all rolled up into one.

It is unreasonable to expect any one person to perform well in all these areas. Jesus Christ is the only person who has ever functioned fully in each role. No wonder so many ministers today are dropping out.

I believe that this is one of the consequences of the church trying to operate with a withered hand of ministry. Most often today "prophets" and "evangelists" are relegated to what is essentially a "parachurch" ministry. Churches bring them in once or twice a year to preach "revival" services and to win a few lost people to Christ, and that's about it. The pastors are expected to bear the brunt of all the rest of the work, and many of them are breaking under the strain. This is why understanding and restoring the five-fold ministry to the Church is so important. We need balance.

Apostles are sent to set things in order. Prophets speak for God to build up the Body. Evangelists declare the good news to the lost. Pastors shepherd, lead, protect, and feed the sheep. Teachers instruct in truth revealing instruction, guidance, enlightenment, doctrine, direction, and knowledge.

The office of the prophet is probably the least-understood and most-neglected ministry office in the Church today. If we refuse to receive an apostle, we refuse order. However, if we refuse to receive a prophet, we refuse destiny. Where there is no destiny there is no future. The Church then becomes relegated to the narrow existence of the here and now. The prophet is the key to the Church's destiny and power.

The Church today needs to recognize and receive the ministry of the prophet and to pray that God will raise those with the prophetic gifting into their proper prophetic office. Those who hold the office of prophet form a charismatic order to which a recognized position should be given in the

Church. A special recognition and authoritative status should be conferred upon those who have manifested certain gifts in a prominent and/or continuing manner. The prophet is the Lord's instrument, one of several means by which Jesus Christ leads His Church. In the power of the Spirit, the prophet manifests the character of the Lord, who is the prophet of the end time.

The Authority of the Prophet

When a prophet is recognized and comes into his office, he brings with him an authority from God that accomplishes two things in the Church. First, it helps us to realize that God is a God of the *now*. A prophet is always reminding us that God *is*, not just that He was; he tells us what God is *doing*, not just what He has done. Knowing what God has done throughout history is important; it is a powerful legacy for us. However, we also need to know beyond doubt that the God of the Bible is the God of today; that the God who blessed Moses, helped David, and anointed Jesus will also bless, help, and anoint us. Our God is a *now* God, and the prophet helps us to remember that.

A prophet has the ability to see things that are not seen. He focuses not on the circumstances, but on the God who rules the circumstances; not on the mess of today, but on the solution that God will provide down the road. The office of the prophet is to speak to us continually in the here and now.

The second thing that the authority of the prophet accomplishes in the Church is that it brings back the fear of the Lord. The sad truth is that there is very little fear of the Lord today either inside the Church or outside. There was a time when a church could be left unlocked 24 hours a day, seven days a week without fear of someone stealing the sound system, vandalizing the building, or spray-painting graffiti on the walls. Now many churches have to allot a significant portion of their budgets to security systems and higher insurance coverage. There was a time when only "essential services" were open for business on Sunday. Now our society treats the Lord's Day as just another day of the week. Gone is the general civic understanding and belief that the nation that honors and serves God will be blessed by God.

Fear of God is lacking in the Church, too. Many believers have only a shallow and immature commitment to God that allows them to constantly rationalize and justify attitudes, behavior, and lifestyles that go against God's will as revealed in His Word. Because there is little understanding of what God expects and requires, there is little fear and a limited sense of awe and respect for His holiness and glory.

The prophet in his office, however, gets our attention and brings us back to a holy fear of God. The Lord is looking for a holy Church, a pure and spotless Bride of Christ. A restoration of the fear of God in the Church is necessary if the Church is to grow into full holiness.

The Marks of a Prophet

There are at least ten distinguishing marks of the prophetic office; these characteristics in the lives and ministries of believers identify them as prophets. These traits should be evident in varying degrees in the life of anyone with a prophetic gifting who is attempting to grow and develop in that gifting. They are most fully developed in those who have been raised into the prophetic office. Whenever we see any of these qualities displayed in someone's life, we should encourage that person to grow and develop their gift.

1. Preaching that exhorts and strengthens the disciples. The prophet's message always builds up the lives of disciples; it never tears down. A disciple is a student; someone who is learning, maturing, and growing up in the Christian faith. These are the ones who are encouraged and strengthened by the prophet's message. Those believers who have refused to mature, on the other hand, may find the prophet's message to be harsh and painful. It always hurts to be outside of the will of God. A prophet's word always builds up those who are striving to grow in Christ.

2. *Character that is true, honest, faithful, and holy.* A prophet points to and reminds us of our destiny in Christ. Therefore, his life should display the character of Christ. While this is true of all believers, it is particularly critical for those in the prophetic office. The Old Testament prophets were held to a very high standard, not only by the people but by God. Moses was a prophet (see Deut. 34:10); yet one lapse on his part in representing God before the people resulted in God denying him the opportunity to enter the Promised Land (see Deut. 32:48-52). Character matters.

3. *A message that appeals not to the flesh but to the spirit.* Growing disciples want messages that challenge and stretch their spirits. Babes in the faith who have no interest in growth usually don't like prophetic preaching because it brings them under conviction. They are more interested in gratifying the flesh. The message of a true prophet always speaks to the spirit directly and without compromise.

4. *Prediction and fulfillment of prophecy.* In other words, a prophet speaks something concerning the future, and God fulfills that prophecy. It could be a prophecy spoken into the life of an individual or an entire congregation. Whatever form it takes, such a prophecy will be specific in nature with clearly measurable fulfillment. Once the event comes to pass we know that God has raised that prophet into office.

5. *Spiritual discernment in the lives of others.* This one sometimes makes people nervous, particularly those who know that their lives are not what they should be in the Lord. A prophet has the ability in the Spirit to discern spiritual reality in the lives of others, good or bad, and speak concerning that reality. This prospect creates anxiety in some people who fear that the prophet will uncover all the mess they have allowed into their lives. Have no fear. A mature prophet will never *publicly* uncover mess because God does not embarrass people. The prophet may address the problem *privately* with the person, if the Lord leads that way. However, he is more likely to exhort the person to follow God's will and obey what God has told him to do.

6. *Declaration of divine judgments when needed.* This is another one that makes people nervous. Sometimes a situation is so bad or has gone on so long that the word of the Lord through the prophet is one of judgment. Prolonged rebellion or disobedience to God, or refusal to heed prophetic warnings or respond to calls for repentance, will ultimately bring about God's judgment. No one likes these kind of pronouncements, least of all the prophet, but sometimes they are necessary.

7. *Willingness to suffer for speaking the truth without saving self.* A mature prophet has long since committed his or her life totally into God's keeping and has recognized that suffering is an "occupational hazard." Speaking the truth for God is more important than personal comfort. Sometimes suffering comes as a result of declaring divine judgment. Jeremiah spoke the truth about God's coming judgment on the southern kingdom of Judah and was convicted of treason and imprisoned in a dry cistern. A true prophet is not afraid to suffer for the truth.

8. *A message in harmony with the Word of God and the known will of God.* A prophet's message will never, repeat

never, contradict the Word of God. The Spirit and the Word always agree. Since a prophet is a "pneumatic" (Spirit-person), his word will also be in agreement with the Word of God. A message that goes against God's Word is a sure indicator of a false prophet.

9.   Employment of symbolic actions. Prophets preach with pictures. Jesus used this method all the time in His teaching, painting pictures in people's minds through the stories and parables He told. Prophets use pictures because that's the way God reveals His will and His Word to them. A prophet sees how things are done in the natural and applies it to the spiritual.

10.   Ability and authority to judge the manifestations of prophetic gifts. A prophet serving in a recognized and acknowledged prophetic office has the ability and authority to identify and judge the presence, display, and use of prophetic gifts in others. In other words, a prophet has the ability to recognize and identify other prophets (both true and false).

Biblical Examples of Prophetic Office

It will be easier to understand the office of the prophet if we look at some biblical examples. The ministries of Elijah, Jeremiah, and John the Baptist are all powerful pictures of the prophet at work.

Elijah

The biblical record of Elijah reveals one important element of prophetic office: declaration. Elijah was always declaring the Word of the Lord. He didn't whine to God; he didn't beg God. He heard from God then declared what he heard. Elijah spoke in faith according to what he heard from God, and it came to pass. The prophetic office is the office of declaration, the ministry of confessing the Word of God.

As a prophet of God, Elijah declared the Word of the Lord.

1.   Elijah declared with a loud proclamation. The first time Elijah appears in Scripture, he confronts Ahab, one of Israel's most wicked kings, with a proclamation from God. "Now Elijah the Tishbite, from Tishbe in Gilead, said to Ahab, 'As the Lord, the God of Israel, lives, whom I serve, there will be neither dew nor rain in the next few years except at my word' " (1 Kings 17:1). Elijah pronounced a drought and there was no rain in Israel for three and a half years.

2.   Elijah declared his righteous position. Several times Elijah declared his status as a servant of God. "As the Lord, the God of Israel, lives, whom I serve…" (1 Kings 17:1b); "As the Lord Almighty lives, whom I serve…" (1 Kings 18:15b); "O Lord…let it be known today that You are God in Israel and that I am Your servant…" (1 Kings 18:36b). Later, he declared to God, "I have been very zealous for the Lord God Almighty" (see 1 Kings 19:10,14).

3.   Elijah declared God's provision. During the drought God instructed Elijah to stay with a widow in the village of Zarephath who would provide him with food. The woman and her son were close to starvation, having only a handful of flour and a little oil. Elijah made her a promise. "For this is what the Lord, the God of Israel, says: 'The jar of flour will not be used up and the jug of oil will not run dry until the day the Lord gives rain on the land" (1 Kings 17:14). The promise was fulfilled. The woman, her son, and Elijah had enough to eat throughout the entire drought. The jar of flour and jug of oil did not run out until the drought was over.

4.   Elijah declared divine confrontation. Elijah challenged the 450 prophets of Baal to a demonstration to reveal whether the Lord or Baal was God of Israel. Each side built an altar on Mount Carmel and sacrificed a bull—the prophets of Baal going first, followed by Elijah. Elijah challenged the prophets of Baal to "...call on the name of your god, and I will call on the name of the Lord. The god who answers by fire—He is God" (1 Kings 18:24a). In the end, the prophets of Baal received no response to their cries and prayers, but God sent fire to consume Elijah's offering and altar. Elijah then had the prophets of Baal put to death.

5. *Elijah declared promised confirmation.* The challenge on Mount Carmel was a result of God's word to Elijah, "Go and present yourself to Ahab, and I will send rain on the land" (1 Kings 18:1b). After the Lord revealed His power and glory on Mount Carmel and the prophets of Baal were executed, "Elijah said to Ahab, 'Go, eat and drink, for there is the sound of a heavy rain'...Meanwhile, the sky grew black with clouds, the wind rose, a heavy rain came on and Ahab rode off to Jezreel" (1 Kings 18:41,45).

6. *Elijah declared complete restoration.* The purpose of the demonstration on Mount Carmel was to restore the people of Israel to faith and obedience toward God. Elijah prayed, "O Lord, God of Abraham, Isaac and Israel, let it be known today that You are God in Israel and that I am Your servant....Answer me, O Lord...so these people will know that You, O Lord, are God, and that You are turning their hearts back again" (1 Kings 18:36b-37). When the Lord responded with fire that consumed the altar as well as the offering, all the people fell on their faces and cried out, "The Lord—He is God! The Lord—He is God!" (1 Kings 18:39b)

7. *Elijah declared glorious abundance.* When Elijah announced the coming of rain, he was not talking about a spring shower but a drenching downpour that would restore the land. "Elijah was a man just like us. He prayed earnestly that it would not rain, and it did not rain on the land for

three and a half years. Again he prayed, and the heavens gave rain, and the earth produced its crops" (Jas. 5:17-18).

Everything that Elijah declared came to pass. We all need to learn to declare in faith like Elijah and see the Word of the Lord come to pass in our lives.

Jeremiah

At the very beginning of the book that bears his name, the prophet Jeremiah describes his prophetic office and calling as he received it from God.

> *The word of the Lord came to me, saying, "Before I formed you in the womb I knew you, before you were born I set you apart; I appointed you as a prophet to the nations." "Ah, Sovereign Lord," I said, "I do not know how to speak; I am only a child." But the Lord said to me, "Do not say, 'I am only a child.' You must go to everyone I send you to and say whatever I command you. Do not be afraid of them, for I am with you and will rescue you," declares the Lord. Then the Lord reached out His hand and touched my mouth and said to me, "Now, I have put My words in your mouth. See, today I appoint you over nations and kingdoms to uproot and tear down, to destroy and overthrow, to build and to plant"* (Jeremiah 1:4-10).

Even before he was born Jeremiah was set apart by God and appointed as a prophet to the nations. Jeremiah did indeed prophesy over not only Israel and Judah but also over the pagan nations that surrounded them. His prophecies spoke of judgment, war, destruction, disaster, exile, and restoration—exactly the kinds of things the Lord had told Jeremiah when He said, "I appoint you...to uproot and tear down, to destroy and overthrow, to build and to plant."

The Office of the Prophet

We are hearing much the same prophetic word in the Church today. The Lord is uprooting those things that are destructive to the Kingdom. He is tearing down demonic strongholds, destroying the power of the enemy, and overthrowing the "strong man" in his own house (see Mk. 3:27). In the name of Jesus we can take away satan's power and authority by reminding him that he was spoiled at Calvary by our elder brother, Jesus Christ; that he is now under the feet of our Lord; and that one day he must bow his knee and confess with his tongue that Jesus Christ is Lord.

All this also results in the planting of the Church and the building up of the Kingdom of God. The enemy is being brought down and the glory of God is rising up within us.

John the Baptist

John the Baptist was the fulfillment of a long-held expectation among the Jews that Elijah would one day return. Jesus made this clear during a discussion with His disciples: "For all the Prophets and the Law prophesied until John. And if you are willing to accept it, he is the Elijah who was to come" (Mt. 11:13-14). John was a prophet in the spirit and tradition of Elijah. He was like a farmer plowing his field. His message broke and turned over fallow ground of barren spirits; his words cultivated the hearts of dry and thirsty men.

John the Baptist was "a voice of one calling in the desert, 'Prepare the way for the Lord, make straight paths for Him' " (Mt. 3:3); the prophet who came as a forerunner to the Messiah, Jesus Christ. He preached a message of repentance and warned the insincere who came to him, "You brood of vipers! Who warned you to flee from the coming wrath? Produce fruit in keeping with repentance" (Mt. 3:7b-8).

Once Jesus appeared on the scene and inaugurated His public ministry, John's mission was completed and he began to fade into the background. He expected this and welcomed it:

> You yourselves can testify that I said, "I am not the Christ but am sent ahead of Him. The bride belongs to the bridegroom. The friend who attends the bridegroom waits and listens for him, and is full of joy when he hears the bridegroom's voice. That joy is mine, and it is now complete. He must become greater; I must become less" (John 3:28-30).

The prophetic ministries of Elijah, Jeremiah, and John the Baptist were for the purpose of turning "the hearts of the fathers to their children, and the hearts of the children to their fathers..." (Mal. 4:6b).

Discerning the Spirits

There are two types of spirits, angelic and demonic, and it is important to be able to distinguish between them. The apostle John addressed this in his first Letter. "Dear friends, do not believe every spirit, but test the spirits to see whether they are from God, because many false prophets have gone out into the world" (1 Jn. 4:1). The implication here is that demonic spirits are the inspiration for the message of false prophets. Part of the true prophet's gifting is a special ability to "test the spirits"; to discern between angelic spirits and demonic spirits.

The writer of Hebrews asked, "Are not all angels ministering spirits sent to serve those who will inherit salvation?" (Heb. 1:14), and Paul told the Corinthians, "The spirits of prophets are subject to the control of prophets" (1 Cor. 14:32). Wherever there is a prophet, there are angels nearby. We find evidence of this in the Old Testament. The fiery chariot that took Elijah up to Heaven was undoubtedly driven by an angel. When Elisha and his servant were in Dothan surrounded by an army sent to capture them, Elisha prayed for his servant's eyes to be opened to see the divine protection God had given them. The servant then "...saw the hills full of horses and chariots of fire all around Elisha" (2 Kings 6:17).

The Gospel of Matthew says that angels ministered to Jesus after His temptation in the wilderness (see Mt. 4:11). According to Luke, Jesus practically stepped right from the desert of temptation into the synagogue at Nazareth, where He declared, "The Spirit of the Lord is on Me, because He has anointed Me to preach good news to the poor. He has sent Me to proclaim freedom for the prisoners and recovery of sight for the blind, to release the oppressed, to proclaim the year of the Lord's favor" (Lk. 4:18-19). What was Jesus doing? He was prophesying. The angels who had ministered to Him had imparted strength and power to Him that He might speak the Word of the Lord prophetically. Later, an angel ministered to Him in the garden of Gethsemane (see Lk. 22:43).

Now if prophets attract angels, they also attract demons because the demons know that if they can prophesy falsely through an individual, they can bring confusion into a church. There are some people who, although they have been saved, nevertheless have given themselves to the dark side of evil, sometimes allowing evil spirits to manipulate their speech. Instead of speaking unity, they speak division; instead of speaking blessing, they speak cursing. Part of the prophetic office is to discern the good from the bad, the angelic from the demonic.

Prophetic Assurance

The Holy Spirit works through the life and ministry of a prophet to produce assurance in the Body. Prophetic assurance is the conviction that accompanies the prophetic understanding and proclamation that every believer is in the process of being prepared by God to serve His purposes. This assurance comes in four areas.

First of all, the prophet's ministry helps us understand that as believers we have been God-*appointed*. Why is that important? There are times in our lives and our walk of faith when the enemy attacks and we get discouraged or confused. In those moments it is easy to let doubt and uncertainty rise up and cause us to question whether or not we are doing the right thing. If the Spirit has planted in our hearts the assurance that we have been appointed by God and are working out His will, that assurance becomes a focal point that helps us keep our bearings. The knowledge that we are God-appointed gives us confidence. If He has appointed us, no effort of man or the enemy can bring us down. Paul says in the eighth chapter of Romans, "If God is for us, who can be against us?" (Rom. 8:31b)

If we are God-appointed, then we can be sure that we are also God-*anointed*. Whomever God appoints He anoints. Just as Aaron and his sons were appointed as priests, so were they then anointed to their office. Just as Saul was appointed king of Israel, so was he anointed king of Israel. When God appointed David to replace Saul as king, He sent Samuel to anoint David. Jesus Christ was appointed to be the Son of God, then was anointed to preach good news.

God does not go back on His decisions. "God is not a man, that He should lie, nor a son of man, that He should change His mind. Does He speak and then not act? Does He promise and not fulfill?" (Num. 23:19) Once God anoints us, He expects us to live the rest of our lives in that anointing. In fact, I am convinced that God never removes the anointing. If, however, we walk outside the will of God, our anointing will become a curse. I do not believe that God ever took away Saul's anointing; He just stripped the kingdom of Israel from him. Saul still had a king's anointing, but without a kingdom it became a curse to him. I am convinced that Judas was anointed by God as one of the twelve, but his anointing became a curse when he betrayed Jesus and tried to deny and destroy that anointing. The pain and the guilt drove him to suicide.

The same kind of thing happens today. Anointed people move away from God and end up miserable. Everything they do seems cursed. They are unhappy, and nothing seems to work out for them because the anointing keeps trying to call them back to where they need to be.

All who are God-appointed and God-anointed must also be God-*approved*. Approval involves being tested or proven. My father is a baker, and through the years I have learned some things from him. For instance, when you are ready to fry doughnuts, you don't just put them directly from the table into the hot grease. They have to spend some time in the "proof box" first. This is a container that warms or "proofs" the dough before frying. If a doughnut is not proofed long enough—if it doesn't stay in the heat long enough—it will be gooey in the middle after frying. We need to be "proofed" sufficiently so that we will be completely "done"—mature.

On the other hand, if a doughnut spends too much time in the proof box it becomes overproofed, and all it will do is soak up grease. Then it becomes soggy and heavy. Have you ever eaten a heavy doughnut, the kind that felt like a ten-pound weight in your stomach? Have you ever known an "overproofed" Christian, someone who didn't want to get out of the "box"? They end up becoming a weight and a burden to everyone.

If we are God-approved we can expect to be tested.

Finally, those whom God appoints, anoints, and approves, He also *assigns.* He sends us out in His name to do His will and to accomplish His purpose in the earth. Jesus said to His disciples, "As the Father has sent Me, I am sending you" (Jn. 20:21b). Someone who is sent by another carries the authority of the sender. An ambassador to a nation speaks for and carries the authority of the government that appointed and assigned him.

As believers our assignment comes from the Lord Himself, the King of kings and Lord of lords, and as we go we carry His authority with us. Satan recognizes that authority and hates it because it means his downfall. We do not stand in our own power or our own authority, but in the power and authority of the Lord, which are sufficient to pull down strongholds.

Prophetic Power

The prophet in his office will also manifest spiritual power in the demonstration of signs and wonders. In other words, wherever there is a prophet, there is power. If there was ever a day that the Church needed prophets and the power that comes with them, it is the day we are living in. The people of our world are desperately searching for an answer to the spiritual emptiness in their souls and the deadness in their spirits. They try everything imaginable: drugs, alcohol, sex, philosophy, religions of all kinds. A growing number seek answers by dialing 1-900-"DEMONIC" to talk to a "professional" psychic, trying to get a devil to give them a reading.

Many of these people have tried "church" and have found it to be as clueless and dead as anything else. They experienced nothing but dead hymns sung by a dead congregation, followed by a dead sermon preached by a dead preacher. The Church is supposed to have the answer. The Church is supposed to have the power. The Church is supposed to make a difference. We will never be as powerful or as effective as we can and should be until we learn to recognize and receive the office of the prophet...indeed, until the entire five-fold ministry hand is fully restored and healthy.

Prophetic Teaching

One of the functions of a prophet is to bring prophetic teaching to the Church. Prophetic teaching involves the typological interpretation of Scripture, which is a "spiritual perspective" of the Christian community. What this means is recognizing that the Word of God is filled with examples—stories lived out on the stage of history—to show God's people an understanding of how God works.

One great example of this is the account in Genesis of Abraham's desire to find a wife for his son Isaac. The story is found in the twenty-fourth chapter of Genesis. Abraham sends his chief servant back to Abraham's homeland and family to choose from his own relatives a wife for Isaac. The servant obeys and finds Rebekah, the granddaughter of Abraham's brother, Nahor. After receiving the hospitality of the family, the servant explains his mission. Rebekah agrees to return with him and is released with the blessing of her family. Upon arriving in Canaan she becomes Isaac's wife.

This seems like just a lovely little story until you understand it prophetically. From the prophetic viewpoint, Abraham is a picture of God the Father, and Isaac, the son of promise, the covenant son, is a type of Jesus Christ. The chief servant is a type of the Holy Spirit. In typological interpretation, the story represents how the Father sent the Holy Spirit to find a bride for the Son. Rebekah is a type of the Church. The chief servant's first meeting with Rebekah is at a well. The only place that the Spirit can find a bride suitable for the Son is at a well where waters are springing up for eternal life forevermore.

The servant bears great gifts to give the bride. The Holy Spirit comes bearing great gifts from the Father for the Church. The gifts of the Spirit are to help us understand how much the Son of God wants us to live with Him forever where there is no death, no pain, no sorrow, and no divorce. However, only a willing bride is acceptable. Rebekah was willing to travel to Canaan to become Isaac's bride. So the chief servant took her back with him.

The Father sent the Spirit to find a bride for the Son. When the Spirit returns to the Son and the Father, He will not return alone; He will bring the Church, the Bride of Christ, with Him. The Word of God says that Isaac was outside sitting on the fence when he first saw Rebekah and the servant approaching. He was watching and waiting with anticipation. As soon as he saw them coming, he got down off the fence.

For the Lord Himself will come down from heaven, with a loud command, with the voice of the archangel and with the trumpet call of God, and the dead in Christ will rise first. After that, we who are still alive and are left will be caught up together with them in the clouds to meet the Lord in the air. And so we will be with the Lord forever (1 Thessalonians 4:16-17).

The Office of the Prophet

That's prophetic teaching, and it usually comes in one of three ways: covenant theology, creation theology, or judgment theology. Covenant theology approaches the whole Old Testament as prophecy—as a shadow of things to come, where the shadow is now becoming reality in this end-time age.

The reality must exist before the shadow. A shadow is only a representation of something fuller and greater. The Book of Hebrews says that the tabernacle was a shadow of the greater heavenly sanctuary that already existed. We can learn certain details about an object from its shadow, but we can only know it fully when we see the real thing. Paul wrote, "Now we see but a poor reflection as in a mirror; then we shall see face to face. Now I know in part; then I shall know fully, even as I am fully known" (1 Cor. 13:12).

So far all we have known has been the shadow, the "poor reflection." As we draw nearer to the end of time, God is giving us a growing understanding of the reality behind the shadow. For we are nearing the day when we will see Him face to face in all His splendor and glory. Then we will not just see a "poor reflection" but will behold Him face to face.

Creation theology focuses on the truth that through Christ, God began a "new creation." Isn't that what Paul said? "Therefore, if anyone is in Christ, he is a new creation; the old has gone, the new has come!" (2 Cor. 5:17) God is preparing a new Jerusalem, a new heaven, and a new earth because the old ones are going to pass away (see Rev. 21:1-2). All history since the fall has been moving toward this end.

Judgment theology means that the Old Testament examples give insight to the present and future judgments of God. Those judgments reveal to us that God is longsuffering and that His mercy endures forever. Over and over He sent judgment on Israel because of their sins. Over and over they repented and returned to Him. Always He restored them. "Because of the Lord's great love we are not consumed, for His compassions never fail. They are new every morning; great is Your faithfulness" (Lam. 3:22-23). Unrepentant hearts face the eternal wrath and judgment of God, but it doesn't have to be so. God does not want to be a God of judgment; He would much rather be a God of mercy.

Dynamic Duo

Ultimately, the office of the prophet serves to declare that Christ is the source of *all* gifts, including the miracle of new life itself. When paired in this function, the prophet and the apostle together form a spiritual "dynamic duo." We find in the Book of Acts that God joined these two offices in the lives of Paul the apostle and Silas the prophet. As they traveled together their ministry multiplied because each of them realized that the other's gift and office were as dynamic and important as his own. Neither was greater than the other; both were needed.

Both the office of the apostle and the office of the prophet are fundamental. Without order, the prophetic gift will lead God's people to fanaticism. Without the prophet, the apostolic gift will lead God's people to so much structure that there is nothing left except form without life.

Chapter Four

Eldership: The Government of God

Paul and Barnabas appointed elders for them in each church and, with prayer and fasting, committed them to the Lord, in whom they had put their trust (Acts 14:23).

As they traveled from town to town, they delivered the decisions reached by the apostles and elders in Jerusalem for the people to obey (Acts 16:4).

The elders who direct the affairs of the church well are worthy of double honor, especially those whose work is preaching and teaching (1 Timothy 5:17).

It's not always easy to be objective when we study the New Testament Church, its government and structure, and the role of the five-fold ministry. All of us are so heavily influenced by the teaching and practice of our particular denominational affiliation that it's difficult to approach the subject with an open mind. Each group is structured and governed according to its own pattern, which the members insist is the best way, the most effective way, the "biblical" way.

Yet, how often do we *seriously* examine the Scriptures to see if our *practice* conforms to the *pattern* God has given in His Word? After all, the Bible is our guide. God's Word is a lamp to our feet and a light to our path (see Ps. 119:105). He has given us patterns and guidelines for everything we need to know about life in the Kingdom of Heaven. Just as God gave His law through Moses to teach the Israelites how to live as His chosen people, and just as He gave Moses the pattern and exact details for the tabernacle so that the people could learn how to worship Him, so Christ gave a precise pattern for the establishment, structure, and government of His Church.

We need to pay close attention to the New Testament pattern of Church government. Jesus is the Head of the Church. He established it, He is building it according to His will, and He alone has the right to govern it. The New Testament pattern of Church government is, in a word, *eldership*. Eldership could be called the "government of God."

The Head of the Church

Understanding New Testament Church government begins with the understanding that Jesus Christ is the absolute Head of the Church. He established it, and it belongs to Him. Jesus said to Peter, "...upon this rock [meaning the revelation of Himself] I will build My church; and the gates of hell shall not prevail against it" (Mt. 16:18 KJV). He didn't say that He would build a Baptist church or a Methodist church or a Pentecostal or Charismatic church. He said, "I will build *My* Church." The only people who are members of *His* Church are those who have submitted

Eldership: The Government of God

themselves through repentance and faith to His salvation and His Lordship.

Membership in Christ's Church does not come by shaking a preacher's hand, by being sprinkled or immersed, or by signing your name on a membership roll. The only criterion is, "that if you confess with your mouth, 'Jesus is Lord,' and believe in your heart that God raised Him from the dead, you will be saved" (Rom. 10:9). Being saved through faith in Christ as Savior and Lord makes us part of His Church. Nothing else will.

If the Church belongs to Jesus Christ, and if He is building it, then clearly He has authority over it. In fact, Jesus Himself said, "All authority in heaven and on earth has been given to Me" (Mt. 28:18b). It is in this authority that Jesus then issued the "mission statement" for His Church: "Therefore go and make disciples of all nations, baptizing them in the name of the Father and of the Son and of the Holy Spirit, and teaching them to obey everything I have commanded you. And surely I am with you always, to the very end of the age" (Mt. 28:19-20).

Jesus is the Head of the Church by the will and purpose of God. In John 5:19 Jesus said that He could do nothing by Himself, but only what His Father did. He established the Church because it was His Father's will. Paul wrote to the Ephesians, "And God placed all things under His [Christ's] feet and appointed Him to be head over everything for the church, which is His body, the fullness of Him who fills everything in every way" (Eph. 1:22-23). Later in the same Letter Paul plainly states, "For the husband is the head of the wife as Christ is the head of the church, His body, of which He is the Savior" (Eph. 5:23).

Anything with more than one head is considered a monster. The Church is not a monster. It has only one Head, Jesus Christ. Authority in the Church is based not on education or religion, not on talent or ability, but on Jesus as Head. He alone is our builder and our authority. He alone is Lord.

Government Through Delegated Authority

Christ governs His Church through delegated authority. The wisdom of delegated authority is affirmed throughout Scripture. Moses became a more effective leader when he learned how to delegate. Every prophet, priest, and king in Israel operated under delegated authority from God. That is why those who abused that authority or misrepresented God came under His severe judgment. Moses' abuse of his authority at the waters of Meribah cost him his opportunity to enter the Promised Land.

The principle of delegated authority is demonstrated very clearly in the earthly ministry of Jesus. Throughout His earthly life Jesus represented the Father and acted under the Father's authority. In turn, Jesus called and appointed 12 men to be His apostles, who would represent Him and act under His authority. They walked with Him, lived with Him, and learned under Him so that they could do the things He did. After Jesus ascended to the Father, He sent the Holy Spirit to lead them into the full knowledge of the truth so that they could continue the work He began and do even greater things than He did (see Jn. 14:12).

Because of this process of delegation, to receive Christ was to receive the Father; and to receive the apostles was to receive Christ. When Jesus was preparing to send the 12 out to preach, He told them, "He who receives you receives Me, and he who receives Me receives the one who sent Me" (Mt. 10:40). On another occasion when He commissioned 72 to go into the nearby towns and villages preaching, Jesus said, "He who listens to you listens to Me; he who rejects you rejects Me; but he who rejects Me rejects Him who sent Me" (Lk. 10:16). That's pretty powerful stuff!

To reject Jesus Christ as the Son of God is to reject God the Father, period. You may accept Buddha, Mohammed, the angel Moroni, or Joseph Smith, but you have still rejected the Father. You may accept licking a crystal or kissing a frog, but you have still rejected the Father. The only way to the Father is through His Son, Jesus Christ our Lord.

Ephesians 4:11-12 says that Jesus gave the five-fold ministry to the Church so that the Church could be built up and brought to maturity. Those who operate in the gifts and offices of the apostle, prophet, evangelist, pastor, and teacher represent Christ and act under His delegated authority. If we reject or refuse to receive any of these, then we reject Christ in those areas. We reject His anointing and His authority. Whenever we reject Christ's anointing in any area, the anointing cannot be applied to our lives and we cannot function where that anointing would take us. That's why so much of the Church has a withered hand. Rejecting the five-fold ministry means rejecting part of who Christ is.

Later on, Jesus expanded His delegated authority beyond the apostles to include *anyone* He sent. "I tell you the truth, whoever accepts anyone I send accepts Me; and whoever accepts Me accepts the one who sent Me" (Jn. 13:20). What this means is that our attitude toward those whom Christ appoints or sends as His delegated authority is the outward and visible expression of our attitude toward Christ and toward the Father. If we reject the one whom God sends, we reject God; if we accept the one whom God sends, we accept God.

Eldership—Christ's Delegated Authority

Ephesians 4:11-12 says that the Lord gave as gifts to the church apostles, prophets, evangelists, pastors, and teachers for the purpose of building and leading the Church into maturity. In the New Testament these appointed gifts are known collectively as elders. The eldership represents Christ's delegated authority for governance and order in His Church. The apostle Peter, writing to church elders, referred to himself as a "fellow elder."

> *To the elders among you, I appeal as a fellow elder, a witness of Christ's sufferings and one who also will share in the glory to be revealed: Be shepherds of God's flock that is under your care, serving as overseers—not because you must, but because you are willing, as God wants you to be; not greedy for money, but eager to serve; not lording it over those entrusted to you, but being examples to the flock* (1 Peter 5:1-3).

This passage also reveals something about the ministry and function of elders. Peter calls them "shepherds of God's flock" and "overseers" who should serve willingly and eagerly as "examples to the flock." Thus we see that elders have a two-fold responsibility in the church: to *rule* and to *teach*.

It will help our understanding of the ruling function of elders to consider three Greek words found in the New Testament that relate to elders and can be translated as "to rule."

The first of these is the word *proistemi*, which means "to stand before, i.e. (in rank) to preside, or (by impl.) to practise:—maintain, be over, rule."[1] This word means to rule in

---

1. James Strong, *Strong's Exhaustive Concordance of the Bible* (Peabody, Massachusetts: Hendrickson Publishers, n. d.), *proistemi*, (G#4291).

the sense of being set over or placed at the head of, as in the husband and father being the head of the family. Referring to an overseer, Paul wrote "He must manage [*proistemi*] his own family well and see that his children obey him with proper respect" (1 Tim. 3:4). Later in the same Letter Paul uses the same word in reference to the work of the elders. "The elders who direct [*proistemi*] the affairs of the church well are worthy of double honor, especially those whose work is preaching and teaching" (1 Tim. 5:17).

The basic sense of *proistemi* has to do with order. It is a priority of *position*. The Scriptures, when referring to the Godhead, always uses the order of Father, Son, and Holy Spirit. While all three are co-eternal and co-existent; omniscient, omnipotent, and omnipresent; and fully equal in essence; the Son and the Spirit have chosen to submit themselves to the Father for the purpose of blessing the earth. Likewise, the order of apostle, prophet, evangelist, pastor, and teacher is a priority of position. The apostle is not greater than the prophet or pastor; he is simply first in order. The pastor is neither greater nor lesser than any of the others. Each is equally important in *function*, but there is a priority of *order*.

Second is the word *hegeomai*, which means "to lead, i.e. command (with official authority); fig. to deem, i.e. consider:—account, (be) chief, count, esteem, governor, judge, have the rule over, suppose, think."[2] This word is used in the understanding of a general leading an army. A victorious army must have an effective leader, and the leader is always the general. A good example of the word used with regard to elders is found in the Book of Hebrews: "Obey your leaders [*hegeomai*] and submit to their authority. They keep watch over you as men who must give an account. Obey them

---

2. *Strong's*, **hegeomai**, (G#2233).

so that their work will be a joy, not a burden, for that would be of no advantage to you" (Heb. 13:17).

The third word for "rule" is *poimaino*, which means "to tend as a shepherd (or fig. superviser):—feed (cattle), rule."[3] A shepherd is one who tends to the flock. First Peter 5:2, one of the verses we looked at above, contains a good example of this word. "Be shepherds [*poimaino*] of God's flock that is under your care, serving as overseers...."

Elders, then, rule as fathers, protecting and providing for the children who are submitted to them. They rule as generals, leading the army of the Lord into battle. Finally, they rule as shepherds, caring for the flock of God.

In addition to ruling, elders also have a responsibility to teach. This involves *exhortation*, which is making urgent appeals, as well as challenging and encouraging the Church; *counsel*, which is giving advice, guidance, or direction according to God's Word; *admonition*, which is advice, encouragement, and warning given in a gentle, earnest manner; and *revelation*, which is uncovering and bringing forth the truth and the will of God as guidance and direction for the Church.

Elders operate under delegated authority from the Lord. Christ alone has authority over His Church. When elders are operating properly they represent the authority of Christ, based on the will and the Word of God.

The Purpose of Eldership Ministry

One of the main purposes for eldership ministry is to provide plurality of leadership. The reason for this is very simple: No one person can do everything; nor should he be expected to. If too few people are trying to do too much of

---

3. *Strong's*, **poimaino**, (G#4165).

the work, the result will be discouragement, confusion, ineffectiveness, and burnout. Perhaps the clearest teaching of this concept in all of Scripture is found in the eighteenth chapter of Exodus. Moses is in the practice of sitting from dawn until dark to hear and judge the needs, problems, and questions of the people, who line up all day long in order to present their cases. Moses' father-in-law, Jethro, observes this and suggests to Moses a better way.

> *You and these people who come to you will only wear yourselves out. The work is too heavy for you; you cannot handle it alone. Listen now to me and I will give you some advice, and may God be with you. You must be the people's representative before God and bring their disputes to Him. Teach them the decrees and laws, and show them the way to live and the duties they are to perform. But select capable men from all the people—men who fear God, trustworthy men who hate dishonest gain—and appoint them as officials over thousands, hundreds, fifties and tens. Have them serve as judges for the people at all times, but have them bring every difficult case to you; the simple cases they can decide themselves. That will make your load lighter, because they will share it with you. If you do this and God so commands, you will be able to stand the strain, and all these people will go home satisfied* (Exodus 18:18-23).

Jethro's counsel is as timely for today's stressed-out, overworked pastors and other church leaders as it was for Moses. Jethro said that unless the leadership and responsibility were spread out, both Moses, God's servant, and the people would wear out. He said that the work was too heavy for one person to handle alone. In addition, the people as a whole would not be properly cared for. If, however, the responsibility was divided and the authority delegated, the servant of

God (and everyone else) would be able to stand the strain. So Moses appointed overseers with varying levels of authority to assist him in ministering to the people, thus establishing one of the most fundamental principles for effective ministry and management.

A properly functioning eldership provides not only plurality of leadership but complete unity of purpose and action. Both plurality and unity are essential. "Paul and Barnabas appointed elders for them in each church and, with prayer and fasting, committed them to the Lord, in whom they had put their trust" (Acts 14:23). Notice in this verse that Paul and Barnabas appointed elders (plural) in each church (singular). This is plurality of leadership. Nowhere in the New Testament is there any reference to one single individual, whether a pastor or whomever, presiding alone over a local church. Elders were to work together in unity to provide effective leadership for the church.

Consider the Trinity as an example. The Godhead of Father, Son, and Holy Spirit governs in plurality but acts in absolute unity. Likewise, each ruling elder must be mutually submitted to the will and purpose of the whole group. However, this does not mean that there is no leader—remember the rule of order and priority of position we discussed earlier. What it does mean is that all the elders work together under the headship of Christ.

Eldership ministry of this type provides significant benefits to the Church. It promotes mutual relationships while encouraging mutual submission. It provides the discipline, correction, and counsel necessary to help make sure that every leader stays on the proper course. In other words, it provides a system of checks and balances. Finally, eldership ministry develops spiritual maturity as each leader learns to submit his or her will at times to the will of the entire group.

Eldership: The Government of God

Qualifications for Eldership

Another look at Exodus chapter 18 reveals seven qualifications for the men whom Moses chose as elders among the people of Israel.

1.   The choice did not depend on natural talent. Moses surely sought God's direction in the selection process. This is at least implied in verse 23 when Jethro says, "If you do this and *God so commands....*" God looks at the heart, not the physical appearance.

2.   Qualified elders were men who feared God; men who loved and worshiped God, who acknowledged Him as King and who took His Word and His law seriously. These men were to be spiritual leaders so they needed to be spiritual men.

3.   Elders were to be trustworthy men; men who could be counted on consistently to carry out their responsibilities with honesty, fairness, and justice.

4.   Elders were to hate dishonest gain. An elder must serve from proper motives—a desire to minister to the needs of people—and be immune to bribes and other temptations to corrupt behavior.

5.   Elders were to be men of spiritual insight. They needed to be sensitive and open to spiritual truth so they could act wisely and render sound judgments.

6.   Elders were to be men who were willing and able to bear responsibility. Leaders always bear greater responsibility than do the people they lead. For this reason, leaders also have a higher degree of accountability. Elders needed to be spiritually mature, emotionally stable, and morally sound.

7.   Elders were to rule over as many as they were qualified for, be that thousands, hundreds, fifties, or tens. This was probably determined by such factors as age, maturity, experience, and spiritual sensitivity.

If you have ever wondered, "What do I have to be to be an elder?" these qualities give you a good idea. In First Timothy 3:1-7, the apostle Paul identifies 15 qualifications for church elders. Paul's list gives further clarification regarding what is expected of elders.

1.   Blameless. This doesn't mean perfect; no one could meet that standard. Blameless means simply that there are no accusations against you; no questions about your character.

2.   The husband of one wife. Put simply, an elder must not be a polygamist.

3.   Vigilant. This means self-control in your personal life and behavior.

4.   Sober. A sober person knows when to be serious and when not to be. This quality does not refer to a somber, unsmiling countenance, but to the possession of proper thinking; to taking life seriously, being balanced in all its parts.

5.   Good behavior. This means being respectable, living an orderly life, and quietly fulfilling your duty.

6.   Given to hospitality. A hospitable person is kind to strangers and a friend to people he meets.

7.   Apt to teach. As we saw earlier, an elder must have the ability to teach others; to tutor or serve directly as a mentor.

8.   Not given to wine. Drunkenness is out of the question for an elder. He exercises self-control in all things.

9.   Not angry. This means not being prone to jealous or vindictive wrath or to bouts of violent rage. An elder is a peaceful person, one who is in control emotionally.

10.   Not greedy for money. An elder "hates dishonest gain" and is a good steward of his possessions.

11. Patient. This means being fair and gentle in every situation, treating every person with dignity and respect.

12. Not a brawler. An elder is not argumentative, contentious, or quarrelsome. Instead, he seeks to make peace wherever possible and pursues it diligently.

13. Not covetous. An elder has his priorities straight; spiritual things come first. He is not caught up in the love of money or the pursuit of wealth for its own sake.

14. Not a novice. Elders must not be new Christians who lack maturity or grounding. They must have the chance to grow and demonstrate spiritual maturity and stability.

15. Having a good name in the community. This means being honorable; having a reputation for honesty and integrity in every area of life.

These qualifications serve also as safeguards for the health and reputation of the church. It is dangerous, both for the church and for the individual involved, to promote any person too soon. Every believer needs time to grow deep and mature in the faith. Putting a new or young believer into a place of high responsibility too soon could have tragic consequences. No one should become an elder or other church leader until he or she has been thoroughly tested in every area of life. We should never hurry this process. As Paul cautioned Timothy, "Do not be hasty in the laying on of hands, and do not share in the sins of others. Keep yourself pure" (1 Tim. 5:22). After all, it is much easier to have a ceremony of the laying *on* of hands than to have a ceremony of the laying *off* of hands!

Recognizing Elders

The biblical process of recognizing and appointing elders may be a little difficult for many of us as Americans to adjust to, accustomed as we are to the democratic process of voting for everything. Once we truly realize that Jesus Christ is the Lord and Head of the Church, we also understand that His Church is not a democracy. He is not going to be voted out of office, nor is He going to resign. He is King of kings and Lord of lords, and He alone has the right to raise up leaders in His Church.

There are three stages in the process of recognizing and appointing elders. First, an elder is called by the Holy Spirit and set apart by Him. Promotion comes from the Lord, not from men. "No one from the east or the west or from the desert can exalt a man. But it is God who judges: He brings one down, He exalts another" (Ps. 75:6-7). God Himself begins to raise up an elder according to His will. In addition, an elder's gifting begins to make room for him. "A gift opens the way for the giver and ushers him into the presence of the great" (Prov. 18:16). Not only does God promote individuals to eldership, but He also goes before them, making room for their ministry.

The second stage is when an elder-to-be is recognized and approved by other elders. First of all, the elders recognize the gifting of God on the person's life. They also see evidence of the person's willingness to serve as the elder-to-be displays the heart of a servant. The elders make note of the person's faithfulness to Christ and His Church and recognize in this one a personal attitude of godliness, holiness, and righteousness.

I am convinced that there are many more elders in the Church at large than are currently serving. One of the reasons for this is that many of these gifted and called-out people are not willing to serve. The only way anyone can become an elder is to be willing to be a servant. In God's

Eldership: The Government of God

Kingdom, no one can be first until he learns to be last. God won't put you at the top until you're happy serving at the bottom. This calls for faithfulness, patience, and a positive attitude. These are the qualities God looks for.

The final stage is when the new elder is recognized and accepted by the congregation. Notice that there is no mention here of the congregation *voting* on the elder. The new elder has already been called and set apart by God and recognized and approved by other elders. The congregation's part is to recognize and accept the elder whom God has raised up in their midst. They should display a willingness to submit to the new elder's authority and to hold him or her in high esteem. The congregation should show honor to a new elder, especially one who preaches the Word.

It doesn't matter how gifted you are, or how thoroughly you have been approved by other elders, if the congregation is not willing to accept and follow you as an elder, you cannot lead them. If you are trying to lead them and they are not following you, then you are just out for a walk. Eldership is not about position as much as it is about relationship. People won't follow you just because you're an elder. They will follow you because you have a relationship with them, and because you're willing to allow the gift of God to manifest through your life to them, thus making a difference in their lives.

Kingdom Government

The government of God—eldership—is Kingdom government. In these last days God is restoring the governing structure of the five-fold ministry in order to build and establish His Church for the days ahead. This restoration involves the ordering, gathering, and establishing of the people of God, in which each office of the five-fold ministry plays a vital role.

1. Ordering the People. This aspect of Kingdom government is the function and goal of the apostolic and prophetic ministries. They establish and proclaim standards of divine order and divine authority in the Church. Therefore, it is a time of preparation, proving, and placement. If the Church is to enter fully into God's purposes and accomplish His will in the earth, then we must be clear about *who* we are, *where* we are going, and *how* we are going to get there. The apostolic and prophetic offices help us to answer these questions and to develop a clear sense of identity.

2. Gathering the People. The evangelistic ministry focuses on gathering people into the Kingdom of God by proclaiming the principles of divine growth and divine enlargement. God has made it clear in His Word that He wants all people to enter His Kingdom. The gathering period therefore is a time of plenty, prosperity, and increase. In many parts of the world today lost people are coming to Christ in record numbers. The evangelistic ministry helps the Church focus on Christ's command to "go into all the world and preach the good news to all creation" (Mk. 16:15).

3. Establishing the People. This is where the pastoral and teaching ministries come into play. They reveal the truths of divine abundance for building and strengthening the Church and of divine ministry for preparing believers for lives of service in Christ's name. It is a time of service, discipleship, and developing maturity. Pastors and teachers help the Church carry out the Great Commission:

Eldership: The Government of God

Therefore go and make disciples of all nations, baptizing them in the name of the Father and of the Son and of the Holy Spirit, and teaching them to obey everything I have commanded you. And surely I am with you always, to the very end of the age (Matthew 28:19-20).

Are you beginning to see how this works? If you are in a church where the elders are functioning in plurality and unity, with each one properly established and in place, and where God has begun to minister through those gifts, there will be a consistent ministry of preparation, proving, and placement; of plenty, prosperity, and increase; of service, discipleship, and maturity. There will be a continual process of Kingdom building. When this happens, Christ Himself is building His Church and the gates of hell will not be able to stand against it.

This kind of Kingdom building is not based on personality or the approval of men, but is Christ building His Church. It is not based on a program or the style of worship music, but is Christ building His Church. If we try to build the Church, then the principalities and powers of the air can war against us and win. When Christ builds His Church, however, the powers of darkness have no authority or strength to stand against it.

Remember, it is not our Church. We are merely the building blocks, the "living stones...being built into a spiritual house to be a holy priesthood..." (1 Pet. 2:5), with all members set in their proper place and functioning in the proper way. We are "a chosen people, a royal priesthood, a holy nation, a people belonging to God..." (1 Pet. 2:9b), whom together are believing with a heart of faith, reaching out to people with a heart of love, and declaring and confessing the Word of God.

God said, "Not by might nor by power, but by My Spirit" (Zech. 4:6b). Kingdom government is the work of the Spirit of God. A healthy, growing, powerful, and effective Church is the work of the Spirit of God. It isn't us at all, but Him, building us up, establishing us in Him, and planting us exactly where He wants us to be.

Not everyone is called by God to be an apostle, is raised up into the prophetic office, or is brought into the evangelistic office, the pastoral ministry, or the teaching ministry. However, each of us *is* called to follow Christ and to serve faithfully wherever He plants us and in whatever ministry He raises us into.

Understanding Kingdom government clears up many things for us and removes a heavy burden. We realize that it isn't about who's the "top dog" anymore, or about who's first or who's the greatest. *Kingdom government is about understanding and becoming the person God wants each of us to be.*

Chapter Five

The Office of the Evangelist

The Spirit of the Lord is on Me, because He has anointed Me to preach good news to the poor. He has sent Me to proclaim freedom for the prisoners and recovery of sight for the blind, to release the oppressed, to proclaim the year of the Lord's favor (Luke 4:18-19).

...Then the owner of the house ordered his servant, "Go out quickly into the streets and alleys of the town and bring in the poor, the crippled, the blind and the lame....Go out to the roads and country lanes and make them come in, so that my house will be full" (Luke 14:21,23).

But you, keep your head in all situations, endure hardship, do the work of an evangelist, discharge all the duties of your ministry (2 Timothy 4:5).

Ollie didn't look like an evangelist. Well into her 70s, her hair almost gone, maybe two teeth left in her mouth, she was about five feet tall and almost as wide. The first time I saw Ollie she was on crutches, hobbling through the door into the church where I was preaching a revival. Yet an evangelist she certainly was.

The small west Texas town had practically dried up and blown away in the years since its glory days as an oil boom town during the 1920s and 30s. The tiny church where we were holding the revival meetings looked as though it was about to do the same. By the time I met Miss Ollie the first night, I had already greeted 19 grumbling, complaining, downcast saints of God as they trooped into the church building as if they had come for a funeral. I thought, *This is really going to be **some** week!*

Then Miss Ollie came in. Looking at her, my first thought was, *I really don't want to talk to this lady.* After 19 "sickly, sorrowful saints" I was already depressed enough. Nevertheless, I stuck out my hand, smiled, and said, "Can I help you in the door?" She declined my help, so I asked, "Well, how are you tonight?" Her reply surprised me.

"I'm just fine, glory to God."

"You are? What makes you think so?" I asked.

"Well, Jesus is alive, and He lives in my heart. He's coming back again, and my name is in the Lamb's book of life. What more could anybody want?"

I started to ask Ollie if *she* wanted to preach that night! Over the next two weeks of revival services I watched quite a contrast in that church. On one side were the 19 sour saints whose favorite song seemed to be "I shall not be moved," or "Everybody will be happy over there" (but not over here!).

Then there was Ollie. She came alone that first night, singing her favorite song, the one she sang every night, "Blessed Assurance, Jesus Is Mine." The second night she brought another lady with her. By the end of the first week

The Office of the Evangelist

she had four or five people with her every night. By the end of the second week she had brought more than 60 people with her, of whom more than 30 had gotten saved. Ollie was an evangelist, pure and simple. With a heart for the lost, she went out and gathered people.

One night she walked up and handed me a dollar bill for an offering. I didn't feel right about it. After all, here was an old woman who lived in a two-room shack and got her clothes from the Salvation Army. How could I take her money? I tried to return it. "Sister Ollie, I can't accept this."

Ollie simply put it back into my hand, then said, "Listen, young man, you can't have a harvest unless you plant seed, and God knows we need a harvest in this city. If you don't let me plant seed, God will get you."

So I took her dollar. Every few nights after that she came down the aisle and stuck another dollar into my hand.

The last night of the meeting, the night Ollie had more than 60 visitors with her, she hobbled down the aisle on her crutches, tears streaming down her face, and stuffed another dollar in my hand. Then she said, "I just want you to know, I was saved in a little Baptist church in eastern Kentucky when I was a kid, and I've served Jesus every day of my life. I've got kids in the ministry, grandkids in the ministry, and now great-grandkids preparing for the ministry. But I want you to know that this has been the greatest two weeks that I've ever had. I don't want to burst your bubble, but it really hasn't been because of your preaching. The Spirit of the Lord has been here, and I've been able to bring my friends to Jesus."

Ollie was still a Baptist and said that she didn't understand about speaking in tongues or falling on the floor. She had never seen it before. I was surprised because I had assumed that she was a member of the little church where I

87

had been preaching. When I asked her she said, "Oh no. This bunch is dead. They couldn't win anyone to the Lord if they wanted to. No one would want what they've got."

"Well, where do you go to church?"

"I go to a Baptist church nearby," Ollie replied. "They're the only ones who will let me bring these kind of people to the church."

She hugged my neck, kissed me, and handed me my dollar; then out the door she went. You see, Ollie was a gatherer, an evangelist.

About six weeks later the pastor of the little church called and told me that Ollie had gone to a convenience store in the middle of the night, and as she was leaving, she had stepped off the curb, was hit by a car, and had died.

I tried to cry for Ollie but I couldn't, thinking about all the joy that was hers when she got Home to see all the people she had won to Jesus. I couldn't cry, remembering that she didn't live in a two-room shack anymore, but in a mansion with walls of jasper along streets of gold. Ollie had traded her Salvation Army hand-me-downs for a beautiful robe with a label that says, "Washed in the blood of the Lamb." I couldn't cry for Ollie, knowing that she was no longer old and no longer crippled.

If I know Ollie, though, she is still singing her song. She sang it the first night and wanted it sung every night. It was the song of her life, a song that could lead other people to Christ; that's why she loved it so much:

Blessed assurance, Jesus is mine;
Oh, what a foretaste of glory divine.
Heir of salvation, purchase of God;
Born of His Spirit, washed in His blood.
This is my story, this is my song;

The Office of the Evangelist

Praising my Savior all the day long.[1]

Evangelism and the Evangelist

The evangelist is a person with the distinctive ministry of bearing the message of the good news of salvation in Jesus Christ. An evangelist's heart is centered around the burden to see lost people brought into a saving knowledge of Christ. That certainly describes Miss Ollie's heart. Another part of the evangelist's ministry involves teaching the members of the Body of Christ how to share their faith. Imparting a passion for the lost is a paramount requirement of those who possess the gift of the evangelist.

As with all the ministry gifts, Christ is the master model. Whenever He commissions "people gifts" (see Eph. 4:11), He equips these set-apart ones to fulfill their calling. Having experienced and proven His own ministry as an evangelist, Jesus Christ can impart and minister to the needs of those whom He calls to this office. To those so called He gives a passion for souls and the knowledge of how to teach the saints to use wisdom and to be good "fishers of men." Evangelists possess a burning desire to see people saved through faith in Christ. They also feel a strong calling to focus the attention of the Church on the plight of lost people, to challenge the Church to reach out to them, and to train Church members to share their faith effectively. Miss Ollie taught by the example of her life. Her example of evangelism in action would put most of us to shame.

In practice, we can see greater and lesser roles emerge in relationship to the ministry *gift* of the evangelist and the ministry *of* evangelism. While certain specially commissioned persons will fulfill the "people gift" of the evangelist, *all* believers are called to the ministry of evangelism—sharing the good news of salvation in Jesus Christ with the lost. The

---

1. Franny Crosby, "Blessed Assurance," public domain.

evangelist leads the way and helps the rest of us learn how to fulfill our calling.

The Nature and Function of the Office

The New Testament contains three related Greek words that are associated with the office of the evangelist. Each word carries a slightly different emphasis from the others. Together they convey a more complete understanding of the nature and function of the office of evangelist.

The Messenger of the Office

The first word is *euaggelistes*. It occurs three times in the New Testament: in Acts 21:8, "...Philip the evangelist, one of the Seven"; in Ephesians 4:11, "It was He who gave some to be...evangelists..."; and in Second Timothy 4:5, "...do the work of an evangelist...." Literally, the word means "a messenger of good" and denotes a "preacher of the gospel." The references in Acts and Ephesians make it clear that this was a distinctive function in the New Testament Church.[2]

Euaggelistes refers specifically to the messenger who holds the office. Acts 21:8 refers to "Philip the evangelist, one of the Seven." Philip was one of the original seven men who were chosen as deacons, as recorded in the sixth chapter of Acts. As he matured spiritually, Philip took on the character, life, and responsibilities of an elder and began to operate within the government of God specifically as an evangelist.

Philip's gifting for this office was resident in his life from before the time of his birth. Psalm 139 says that God knows all about us before we are born and that all our days are writ-

---

2. W. E. Vine, Merrill F. Unger, and William White, Jr. *Vine's Complete Expository Dictionary of Old and New Testament Words* (Nashville: Thomas Nelson, Inc., Publishers, 1985), ***evangelist***, 208.

ten in His book before we live any of them. Isaiah 49 speaks of God's calling on one's life coming even before birth. What this means is that the call and gift of an evangelist were on Philip from the beginning of his life, even before he became a Christian.

The gift was resident in Philip prior to his conversion, even though it was not operating. Once Philip gave his heart to Christ, however, the gift began to manifest in his life. A strong desire to win the lost grew up very naturally in his heart. It was the most natural thing in the world for Philip to go out and witness and win lost people to Jesus Christ because that's where his heart was. The gifting of the evangelist was operating in his life.

As Philip's evangelistic ministry developed and matured, God molded his character, shaped the call on his life, and eventually moved him into the office of evangelist. The congregation recognized Philip's ministry, as did the other elders. They saw God's hand on Philip's life and accepted him as one whom God was elevating into the office of evangelist.

So *euaggelistes* refers to the *messenger* who holds the office; one whose call and commission have come from God.

The Message of the Office

Euaggelion, the second word, stresses the *message* of the office of evangelist. Occurring 77 times in the New Testament, it is most often translated as "gospel." The word literally means "good message" and "denotes the 'good tidings' of the kingdom of God and of salvation through Christ, to be received by faith, on the basis of His expiatory death, His burial, resurrection, and ascension."[3]

---

3. *Vine, **gospel**, 275.*

The messenger may change, but the message stays the same. Evangelists come and go, but their message never changes. From generation to generation since the first century, true evangelists have preached an identical message. It doesn't matter whether you are Baptist, Methodist, Church of God, Assembly of God, Independent, non-denominational, or multi-denominational; or whether you're male or female, young or old; if you are an evangelist, your message will be the same: salvation by faith in Jesus Christ on the basis of His death, burial, and resurrection.

Just as order comes out of the office of the apostle, and destiny and purpose out of the office of the prophet, so salvation comes out of the office of the evangelist. Can you see the balance? In the Church we need order and we need purpose and destiny; we also need for salvation to be proclaimed to the lost.

The Ministry of the Office

The third word, *euaggelizo*, essentially means "to preach" and stresses the *ministry* of the office of evangelist. It is found in the New Testament 90 times. The literal meaning of the word is "to bring or announce glad tidings;"[4] it "is almost always used of 'the good news' concerning the Son of God as proclaimed in the gospel."[5] The business of the evangelist (*euaggelistes*) is to preach (*euaggelizo*) the "good news" (*euaggelion*) of Jesus Christ.

Evangelists have a great ability to see the good in everyone, even in those who have been written off by everyone else. They are like people who hate to throw anything away. Even if something's old or can no longer be used for its intended

---

4. Vine, *gospel*, 276.
5. Vine, *preach*, 481.

The Office of the Evangelist

purpose, if it is still in good shape some people will want to keep it. "After all," they say, "it's still good. We may find a use for it someday." Are you this type of person, or do you know someone who is? Are you always looking for the good in things, circumstances, and events? That's the way an evangelist looks at people.

No matter who a person is, no matter what he has done, no matter how he acts or lives, no matter how much of a "loser" or a hopeless case an individual may seem to be, an evangelist sees that man or woman, boy or girl, as salvageable. He sees these defeated, overlooked "losers" as people with potential. An evangelist sees people as they *may* become some day instead of focusing on who they *are* at the present time. In other words, evangelists see people the way Jesus sees them.

Jesus was the master evangelist. He saw the potential in every person He met. One day when His disciples tried to turn away some children, He said, "No, you don't understand; they're salvageable" (see Mt. 19:13-15). The unclean, outcast woman with a hemorrhage touched Jesus' robe, and while others would have ignored her or turned her aside, Jesus said, "No, you don't understand; she's still salvageable" (see Mt. 9:20-22). Tiny Zacchaeus, the hated tax collector, received Jesus into his home with joy because unlike the tax collector's neighbors, Jesus saw potential in him. When Jesus called Zacchaeus down from the tree, it was as though He was saying, "Zacchaeus, you are still salvageable" (see Lk 19:2-6). Blind Bartimaeus, calling out to Jesus from the side of the road, was told by the crowd to be quiet, but Jesus said, "No, you don't understand; he is still salvageable. He may be a blind beggar who is worth little or nothing to society, but he is of great worth to Me" (see Mk. 10:46-52).

In his wonderful book *No Wonder They Call Him The Savior*, Max Lucado relates a story from Anthony Campolo of two thieves who broke into a department store one night. Rather than stealing anything, however, they simply switched many of the price tags, putting the tags from low-priced items onto high-priced items, and vice-versa. The thieves then returned to the store the following day with thousands of dollars to purchase the items at prices much lower than they were worth. In the end their greed led to their downfall.[6]

Max Lucado then drew the analogy of how the same thing has happened in our society. Someone has switched the price tags. Professional athletes are paid millions of dollars to play their sport while many schoolteachers have to work a second job just to make ends meet. Greed is often rewarded in our day, while honesty, character, and integrity are played down. Some human life is less highly valued than others: the unborn, the retarded, the old, and the infirm. Someone has switched the price tags.

For this reason we desperately need the evangelist to keep reminding us that every person is important to God. Even if they ring up "zero" on society's cash register, they are still of great worth to God. Jesus died for *all* people. His death paid the sin price for everyone. It's not the price we put on people that makes them salvageable, but the price *the Father* puts on them; and He has said that the blood of Jesus Christ cleanses *every person* from unrighteousness.

The evangelist speaks *hope* into the Church and into society. His office, ministry, and message in one word is *hope*. Everyone needs hope. Our families need it; our churches

---

6. Max Lucado, *No Wonder They Call Him The Savior* (Sisters, Oregon: Multnomah Publishers, 1986), 29-30.

need it; our world needs it. People everywhere are crying out for hope. The true evangelist proclaims hope wherever hope is needed.

Evangelist or Revivalist?

The function of the office of the evangelist is, first of all, to evangelize the lost. That's logical enough. The next part, although not as familiar, is just as important...and probably more so. An evangelist also has the function of teaching the saints how to share their faith. The only way to do this effectively is to impart to them a passion for the lost.

I have often said, "Tell me who you run with and I'll tell you who you are." An old-timer once said, "If you run with a skunk long enough, pretty soon you'll start to smell like a skunk." I'm absolutely convinced that if you run with people who love to win souls, then it won't be long before you too will love to win souls. If you're around folks very long who love to get people saved, it just rubs off.

Any confusion today over the role of the evangelist may be due in part to a misunderstanding of the difference between an evangelist and a revivalist. Those who travel from church to church ministering primarily to the saints, rather than witnessing to the lost, are not evangelists, but revivalists. Many of these are the people we bring in once or twice a year to preach "revival" meetings. These preachers are called "evangelists" by tradition, even if their primary purpose or result is to build up the saints. In reality they are prophets with the gift of exhortation. Mistakenly calling these preachers "evangelists" may allow the church to believe that they have fulfilled their role in evangelism simply because they had a "revival" meeting.

One of the most common questions asked about a revival, even by pastors, is, "How many people were saved?"

Now I don't want to put too fine a point on this, but strictly speaking, a "revival" is not primarily about saving lost people. It is about getting the saints alive enough to do the work of evangelism themselves and to get them ready to handle the situation when people do get saved. Lost people are dead in their trespasses and sins, according to the apostle Paul (see Eph. 2:1-5). In order for anything to be *re*vived there must be life there in the first place. If you go out and win the lost, then bring them into a dead church, it's like pouring new wine into old wineskins. Pretty soon these new saints will begin to wonder what's wrong with the older ones who are sitting around like deadbeats.

Revival is important to the Church; the ministry of the prophet is needed. However, the ministry of the prophet is not the same as the ministry of the evangelist. True prophets build up the family of God by encouraging and exhorting the saints to walk faithfully with the Lord. True evangelists win the lost to Christ and teach the saints how to function in this vital ministry.

The Heart Flow of the Evangelist

If you observe the life of an evangelist and listen to his words for very long, you will begin to see a pattern emerge. Certain emphases that are the outflow of his heart begin to become evident.

1.   The emphasis on the value of an eternal soul. Of all the five-fold ministry offices, the evangelist is the most concerned about eternity. The apostle talks about the here and now and lays the track, while the prophet talks about where we're going here on earth. The evangelist, on the other hand, keeps saying that none of that matters if you don't get saved. Being saved has to do with the here-and-now and

The Office of the Evangelist

with eternity, but the evangelist focuses on the eternal aspect. It has been said that you can be so heavenly minded that you're no earthly good. However, it is also true that if you are not heavenly minded, then you are no earthly good.

2. The emphasis on preaching the Word of God, Jesus Christ, and the Kingdom. When an evangelist preaches, he always talks about the cross, repentance, and faith in Jesus Christ. In a word, he preaches *salvation*. When Paul first preached to the Corinthians, he had a simple, sharply-focused message: "When I came to you, brothers, I did not come with eloquence or superior wisdom as I proclaimed to you the testimony about God. For I resolved to know nothing while I was with you except Jesus Christ and Him crucified" (1 Cor. 2:1-2).

Preaching salvation to the saved is a bit like a vacuum cleaner salesman who sells a machine to a household one day and returns to the same house the next day, trying to sell another one. The Church needs to work hand in hand with the evangelist to make sure that lost people are brought in for him to reach out to.

3. The emphasis on trust may bring a lack of spiritual discernment. What I mean is that an evangelist is more concerned with getting people into the Kingdom of God than with getting the mess in their lives cleaned up. In the eighth chapter of Acts, Philip the evangelist was preaching in Samaria with great success. Many people were being saved. One of these was a magician and sorcerer named Simon, who for a long time had enjoyed much attention and acclaim in the city. Simon believed and was baptized; he then followed Philip everywhere, amazed at the signs and wonders Philip was performing. It was not until Peter and John arrived and Simon tried to buy the miracle-working

97

power from them that the bitter, unrighteous, and sin-enslaved nature of Simon's heart was revealed. Simon had believed, which was what Philip was after, but his life was still messed up in many ways. Philip did not discern the heart of Simon the sorcerer until the apostles Peter and John came to Samaria (see Acts 8:5-24).

Now there is no right or wrong here. Philip was not wrong; neither were Peter and John. It was a matter of a different gifting, ministry, and office. The focus in Philip's heart and mind was to get people saved. Once they were saved, they could be turned over to others who would help them understand and grow. So Philip was interested in getting Simon saved; Peter was interested in getting Simon straightened out.

4.   *The emphasis on public repentance, including baptism.* Billy Graham is the best-known evangelist in the world. He is a true evangelist. The primary focus of all his messages and of all his crusades worldwide is to get people into the Kingdom of God. Through his more than 50 years of ministry, millions have trusted Christ. Every meeting, every message, ends with an appeal for people to respond to Christ—not just quietly in their hearts while standing in place, but boldly, in front of God and everyone else. It's important that those who respond to the good news of Jesus publicly show that they truly mean business with God.

Now of course this scenario is played out on a much smaller scale every week in thousands of churches. The "invitation," the "altar call," or whatever it is called in various churches, is a vital part of making an initial response to Christ. A public stand helps solidify the decision. The most clearly biblical form of public response and testimony is baptism. Evangelists love to use the Scripture that says, "Whosoever therefore shall confess Me before men, him will I confess also before My Father which is in heaven. But whosoever shall deny Me before men, him will I also deny before My Father which is in heaven" (Mt. 10:32-33 KJV).

5. The emphasis on the supernatural power of God to validate the good news. When we hear the words "the supernatural power of God," many of us, particularly the Pentecostals among us, think of limbs straightening out and blind eyes opening. While these are certainly evidence of God's miraculous power, the greatest supernatural sign of all is the changed life and reborn nature of someone who has just been saved. There is no greater miracle than of a dead person being brought to life; of one who was dead in trespasses and sin being made alive in Christ. Evangelists preach Christ with signs and wonders following to confirm and validate the message.

6. The emphasis on passion instead of position. True evangelists are willing to do whatever it takes to win people into the Kingdom of God. Paul wrote in Philippians that Christ "...did not consider equality with God something to be grasped, but made Himself nothing, taking the very nature of a servant, being made in human likeness. And being found in appearance as a man, He humbled Himself and became obedient to death—even death on a cross!" (Phil. 2:6-8) Christ did not consider His position or His crown so precious that He was not willing to lay them aside in order to bring lost humanity back to the Father. Paul wrote of himself, "I have become all things to all men so that by all possible means I might save some" (1 Cor. 9:22b). Evangelists don't care about position or protocol. Their passion is to win souls.

7.   The emphasis on reminding the Church that Jesus Christ came "to seek and to save that which was lost." The apostle believes that Christ came to set things in order. The prophet believes that Christ came to get our lives straightened out. The pastor believes that Christ came to love us, cuddle us, and tell us how wonderful we are. The teacher believes that Christ came to bring us to maturity. The evangelist believes that Christ came to save us. All of these are true, but getting saved is the starting point from which all the others take off.

Searching for Signs of Life

For far too long the Church as a whole has failed to recognize, accept, and honor the office of the evangelist. Evangelistic ministry has been devalued, and in many cases the individual evangelistic gift has been virtually ignored. Focusing on their own problems and needs, churches have turned inward rather than outward. As a result, they have become stagnant: There are few, if any, new spiritual births, and very little dynamic spiritual life can be found. Sadly, many churches today are little more than religious nursing homes tending to the increasingly demanding needs of ailing and immature saints, many of whom have never progressed beyond infancy.

The evangelist helps us keep our focus outward to the needs of a lost world. Whenever a church loses that focus it loses its reason for existing. Understanding that outward focus is the key to understanding the heart of the evangelist. By their words, lives, example, and ministry, evangelists continually remind us that there is more to serving God than worship services, preaching, and all the other things we associate with church. When we get to Heaven, it won't matter how many songs we sang or how many sermons we listened to. The important issue will be how many souls we brought with us; how many people who are in Heaven because we took the time and the opportunity to share Christ with them.

Whether or not evangelism is our specific gift, we have a responsibility before God to support it financially and prayerfully. Church, we need to make evangelism a priority in our planning, our programs, and our prayers, remembering always that the reason Christ came was to seek and to save the lost.

The apostle establishes order in the Church and blazes a trail for the Church to follow. The prophet puts the Church in touch with its destiny and helps it define its purpose. The evangelist helps fill the ranks with new life, with new believers who are just getting started on the road of faith. Who will guide these new ones into maturity and effective service and ministry in the Kingdom of God? That important responsibility rests primarily on the shoulders of the two remaining offices of the five-fold ministry: the pastor and the teacher. The pastor helps believers grow into wholeness, while the teacher helps them grow into discipleship.

Chapter Six

The Office of the Pastor

Keep watch over yourselves and all the flock of which the Holy Spirit has made you overseers. Be shepherds of the church of God, which He bought with His own blood (Acts 20:28).

Be shepherds of God's flock that is under your care, serving as overseers—not because you must, but because you are willing, as God wants you to be; not greedy for money, but eager to serve; not lording it over those entrusted to you, but being examples to the flock (1 Peter 5:2-3).

Pastors are under attack today as never before. Overworked, underpaid, and stressed-out, many of these shepherds of God's flock are crumbling under the weight of unrealistic expectations and the pressure of trying to deal with an almost constant flow of crisis situations in their churches and in the lives of individual church members. Many churches demand more from their pastors than any one person could ever hope to fulfill. Moreover, most pastors would probably agree that the *reality* of ministry is quite different from the *ideal* that they envisioned when they first began.

I fear that there is a growing number of pastors today who would identify with the words of Isaiah as expressing the essential reality of their ministry: "I have labored to no purpose; I have spent my strength in vain and for nothing" (Is. 49:4b). They have counseled people, ministered to people, and responded to needs at all hours of the day and night. They have given of their time, their money, and their wisdom. They have done everything they know to do, yet they feel that they have very little to show for their efforts. The strain is tremendous; the gain, minimal.

In a recent survey of American pastors, 70 percent of respondents indicated that they would leave the pastorate if a viable opportunity opened up in another field. I am convinced that one of the biggest reasons for this dissatisfaction is that they feel they have poured their time, their money, their energy, their heart, and their soul into the Church and have received little in return.

One of satan's chief objectives is to destroy the Church, and with this in mind he makes pastors special targets for attack. This is why it is so important to constantly hold them up in prayer. Quite often, however, unless a pastor makes known a particular request or a specific need, many people do not know how or what to pray for him on a regular basis. Understanding the ministry and office of the pastor will lead both to a greater appreciation of his role in the Church and to better-informed, more specific prayer offered up on his behalf.

Shepherd of the Flock of God

Our English word "pastor" comes from the Latin word *pastor*, which means "herdsman." The only occurrence of

The Office of the Pastor

the word in the English New Testament is in the plural, in Ephesians 4:11: "It was He who gave some to be apostles, some to be prophets, some to be evangelists, and some to be pastors and teachers." The Greek word is *poimen*, which occurs a total of 18 times in the New Testament and literally means " 'a shepherd, one who tends herds or flocks' (not merely one who feeds them)."[1] Aside from Ephesians 4:11, in every instance *poimen* is translated as "shepherd" or "shepherds." One of the most familiar verses using *poimen* is John 10:11 where Jesus said, "I am the good shepherd [*poimen*]. The good shepherd [*poimen*] lays down His life for the sheep."

The verb form of *poimen* is *poimaino*, which is found 12 times in the New Testament and means "to act as a shepherd."[2] *Poimaino* is used in Acts 20:28, "Be shepherds of the church of God..." and in First Peter 5:2, "Be shepherds of God's flock...."

The Hebrew equivalent in the Old Testament is the word *ra'ah*, which means "to pasture, shepherd....Used metaphorically, this verb represents a leader's or a ruler's relationship to his people."[3] As a noun the word means "shepherd" and is usually applied to God as the Great Shepherd who feeds His sheep.[4] By far the most familiar usage of this word is in Psalm 23:1, "The Lord is my shepherd...."

This brief word study makes it clear that a pastor is a "shepherd" who is entrusted with the ministry of tending

---

1. W. E. Vine, Merrill F. Unger, and William White, Jr. *Vine's Complete Expository Dictionary of Old and New Testament Words* (Nashville: Thomas Nelson Inc., Publishers, 1985), **pastor**, NT 462.
2. Vine, **feed**, NT 231.
3. Vine, **to shepherd**, OT 227.
4. Vine, **to shepherd**, OT 228.

the flock of God—with feeding, guiding, and superintending them. This role as a keeper of the flock has a time-honored tradition dating back to the earliest days of the biblical record. Ancient Hebrews understood that a shepherd did more than simply feed the sheep under his care. He was also responsible to oversee the affairs of the sheep and to tend to their physical well-being, including protecting them from predators and robbers. A good shepherd would even give his life to protect his sheep.

This same, all-encompassing care for the flock was carried over into the New Testament understanding of the pastor, with Jesus as the example. "I am the good shepherd. The good shepherd lays down His life for the sheep" (Jn. 10:11). For the most part, as a pastor rules his home, so will he rule the sheep. Pastors who genuinely love the Lord and who love their spouses and children will also genuinely love the sheep whom God has entrusted to their care. As they guard the sheep as Christ's watchmen, they are guarding the most precious thing ever created—the eternal souls of men, women, and children, which are so precious that God gave His Son to redeem them.

Pastors need to appreciate the unique call that God has placed upon them. The Church, too, needs to appreciate, support, and uplift the pastor in his God-given call. Few can genuinely and adequately fulfill the daunting responsibility of the pastoral office unless they are divinely called and graced to do so.

How Do You Train Sheep?

According to the apostle Paul, the five-fold ministry of apostle, prophet, evangelist, pastor, and teacher exists "to prepare God's people for works of service, so that the body of Christ may be built up until we all reach unity in the faith and in the knowledge of the Son of God and become mature, attaining to the whole measure of the fullness of Christ" (Eph. 4:12-13). The purpose and goal of the five-fold ministry is to mature and train the saints of God to do the work of the ministry. The Greek word for "works" in verse 12 is *ergon*, which means to toil with effort or as an occupation, or to labor.[5]

So the office of the pastor (shepherd) exists to help train the people (sheep) to labor faithfully in the ministry. I believe that in the pastor's case this training is accomplished not so much through *words* of instruction as through a *lifestyle* of instruction. A passage from Isaiah serves as a good illustration of this process.

> *Listen to Me, you islands; hear this, you distant nations: Before I was born the Lord called Me; from My birth He has made mention of My name. He made My mouth like a sharpened sword, in the shadow of His hand He hid Me; He made Me into a polished arrow and concealed Me in His quiver. He said to Me, "You are My servant, Israel, in whom I will display My splendor." But I said, "I have labored to no purpose; I have spent My strength in vain and for nothing. Yet what is due Me is in the Lord's hand, and My reward is with My God." And now the Lord says—He who formed Me in the womb to be His servant to bring Jacob back to Him and gather Israel to Himself, for I am honored in the eyes of the Lord and My God has been My strength—He says: "It is too small a thing for you to be My servant to restore the tribes of Jacob and bring back those of Israel I have kept. I will also*

---

5. James Strong, *Strong's Exhaustive Concordance of the Bible* (Peabody, Massachusetts: Hendrickson Publishers, n. d.), **ergon**, (G#2041).

make you a light for the Gentiles, that you may bring My salvation to the ends of the earth" (Isaiah 49:1-6).

Verse 2 of this passage describes the process of arrow-making, a careful and deliberate procedure that requires great patience. Israel is depicted as the Lord's "polished arrow" through which He wants to reveal His glory to the nations. I believe that a good pastor operating in his office will regard his ministry in a similar manner and look at his "sheep" in the same light.

In the Shadow of His Hand

One of the first qualities required for successful arrow making is *patience.* High quality, dependable arrows cannot be made in haste. It takes time. In fact, in Old Testament days, a good archer began to make an arrow a full year before he expected to need it. First, he had to find the right kind of wood. Israelite archers generally used almond branches for their arrows because almond trees had the straightest branches of any tree in Israel.

Once a suitable branch was found, the next step was to strip off the bark and shape and condition the wood by sanding it. This would remove knots, burrs, and anything else that would get in the way of the arrow's purpose. After an initial period of sanding, the wood was soaked thoroughly in water, then removed in order to bring the grain to the surface of the wood. Further sanding followed, and then more soaking and more sanding, until the shaft was the right size, shape, and texture. It was a slow, patient process that was neither glamorous nor exciting, but was necessary for producing high quality arrows.

Pastoring requires the same approach. New believers come into the church "in the rough" and the pastor patiently, steadily, gently, and lovingly sands them with the Word of God and soaks them with the Spirit of God. The Word of God works to remove their "rough edges" and to shape them into "straight arrows" useful to the Lord. The soaking of the Spirit brings their "grain"—the inner workings, thoughts, and imaginations of their hearts—to the surface so the Word can continue to sand them further.

Sanding and soaking the saints is seldom stimulating work. After all, apostles get to raise the dead...and that's exciting. Prophets get to call the people forward...and that's exciting. Evangelists get to see lots of people getting saved...and that's exciting. But the pastor? He devotes his time faithfully and patiently to sanding and soaking, sanding and soaking, sanding and soaking....

A Polished Arrow

The desired end of all this patient labor is a "polished arrow," and attaining the desired end requires giving proper attention to the *process*. Cutting corners or skipping steps will lead to inferior arrows. Process is important. Everything we do in life involves process. Growth is a process, learning is a process, maturing is a process. You don't teach calculus to first-graders; you begin with the basics: 1+1=2, 2+2=4. The same is true in the spiritual realm. "Whom shall He teach knowledge? And whom shall He make to understand doctrine? Them that are weaned from the milk, and drawn from the breasts. For precept must be upon precept, precept upon precept; line upon line, line upon line; here a little, and there a little" (Is. 28:9-10 KJV). God, too, is interested in process.

One of the problems with the Church today, especially in America, is our focus on "event theology." This theology asserts that when we pray or when someone lays hands on us, we can expect everything that is wrong in our lives to be cleared up in a split second with no worry and no waiting. Saints of God, my experience is that God doesn't generally work that way. As a matter of fact, I've *never* seen Him work that way. A work of healing or deliverance may come in a moment, but character development takes a lifetime. It's a process. That's the problem with sanctification; it's so "daily." We have to *die* daily in order to *live* daily; to take up our cross daily in order to walk in the Spirit daily. There are no shortcuts.

A patient pastor is concerned with the process. That's why he keeps on sanding and soaking the saints. He wants to make sure that they reach maturity, "attaining to the whole measure of the fullness of Christ" (Eph. 4:13b).

Concealed in the Quiver

Once the sanding and soaking were completed the arrow shaft was placed in the archer's quiver, a place of *protection.* The quiver was also a place of waiting, a place of proving. Over a period of time, the archer watched to see whether or not the shaft would begin to bow or warp. That is, before he added the arrowhead or the fletching to the shaft, he needed time to see if his new arrow was going to stay straight.

Would you agree with me that it's tough to stay straight when you're "in the quiver"? Sometimes it's dark; sometimes we feel alone; sometimes we become impatient to leave the quiver and get to work. Maturing, testing, and proving take time. After all, Moses was "in the quiver" for 80 years before he was ready for the work God was preparing him for.

The quiver affords protection. Most folks want to jump out of the quiver before it's time. One reason is because they don't realize that the quiver is for their own protection. Many people jump into ministry too soon because they are *pushed* rather than *led*. What pushes them? Impatience, ambition, family, the desire for fame, the desire for money, ego; all these can seduce saints to quit the quiver too soon.

When this happens the believer is like an arrow shaft that is removed from the quiver before it has completed its process. The archer puts the feathers on the arrow, followed by the arrowhead, which he then sharpens. Since the arrowhead is heavier than the rest of the arrow (so that the arrow will fly straight when it leaves the bow), these steps are the final test of the arrow shaft. If the arrow has not been in process long enough, the weight of the arrowhead will cause it to bow, making it very hard to hit the target.

On the other hand, an arrow that stays straight when the feathers and the arrowhead are attached to it is ready to be fitted to the bow and fired. Notice, however, that the arrow does not fit itself to the bow. The archer selects it and releases it to do its job. In the same way, pastors have the responsibility of keeping believers "in the quiver" until they have finished the process—until they have grown and matured to the point where they are ready to be released into ministry. It is the pastor's gift and role to know when the time is right.

A gifted pastor will come to know his people so well that he can tell when they are ready for ministry. This is a matter of critical importance. If the pastor releases someone into ministry and the believer cracks under the stress or misses the mark because of immaturity, his purpose is lost. He will not be a light to the nations.

A Light to the Nations

The purpose of an arrow is to hit the target intended by the archer. We are God's arrows and our target is the world. We dare not choose our target or determine when our ministry is to begin. This is God's prerogative. He alone knows where and what our ministry is to be, and how we are to fulfill His purpose. Like arrows shot by the archer, we are sent by the One who said, "It is too small a thing for you to be My servant to restore the tribes of Jacob and bring back those of Israel I have kept. I will also make you a light for the Gentiles, that you may bring My salvation to the ends of the earth" (Is. 49:6b).

Some "arrows" want nothing more than simply to enjoy the flight; to feel the wind brushing their faces and flowing through their feathers. This is never what God wants. If an arrow fails to hit its target, it fails to fulfill its purpose. Everything it went through—the sanding, the water, the waiting—is useless if it misses the mark. Believers who launch *themselves* into ministry before they are ready stand in great danger of missing the mark and of failing to fulfill God's purpose for them. This is why the office of the pastor is so important. We need to be willing to allow our pastors to come alongside us, to instruct us, and to impart into our lives so that we can understand where we are in the process and know when we are ready to be fitted to the bow. If we don't, and we're shot too soon, we will miss the mark.

Sadly, this sometimes happens to believers. When it does, the reaction of many people is just to write off the one who failed. God doesn't do that, however. He is the God of the second chance, and the third, and the fourth…. If He shoots us, or if we try to shoot ourselves, and we miss the mark, He doesn't just leave us out there on our own; He comes looking for us. He loves us too much and has invested too much in us to abandon us. He seeks to rescue and restore us so that we can still fulfill His purpose to reach the nations. The office of the pastor exists to promote, coordinate, and carry out this ministry of reclaiming, restoring, feeding, and caring for the saints.

The Office of the Pastor

Training Up Shepherds

As sheep all of us are called to follow Jesus, the Great Shepherd. Only a few are then called to become shepherds. These chosen few particularly need a mature pastor because the office of the pastor serves to train sheep to be shepherds. This dichotomy of being both a sheep and a shepherd requires pastors/shepherds to walk a fine line with one foot in each of two worlds. Just as with arrow-making, the transformation from a sheep to a shepherd involves a process, which is clearly illustrated in Psalm 23.

Beginning the Process—Being a Sheep

The Lord is my shepherd; I shall not want. He maketh me to lie down in green pastures: He leadeth me beside the still waters. He restoreth my soul: He leadeth me in the paths of righteousness for His name's sake (Psalm 23:1-3 KJV).

One of the first qualifications required of anyone who is operating in the office of the pastor/shepherd is the ability to maintain his perspective as a sheep. One who is to train sheep to be shepherds must continue to see himself as a sheep of Jesus, the Great Shepherd. "The Lord is *my* shepherd; I shall not want." "We are His people, and the sheep of His pasture" (Ps. 100:3b KJV). If we are His sheep, then He is our Shepherd.

Sheep know and trust their shepherd. As sheep, believers must therefore say, "I have a shepherd; the Lord is *mine*." This truth stresses *relationship*. He is our shepherd. We did not buy Him; He bought us. We did not choose Him as much as He chose us. We do not have a hold on Him as much as He has a hold on us. Because the Lord has chosen us and holds on to us, we can say with joy, "I am His and He is mine!"

113

A second truth we can claim as sheep is the truth that "I shall not be in want; the Lord is Jehovah-Jireh" (see Gen. 22:14). Our Shepherd is God, our Provider. This does not mean bare subsistence living. When God provides, He provides abundantly. As our Shepherd He leads us into places where there is not only food to eat but also more than enough be filled. He sets out a heavenly buffet.

With the Lord as our Shepherd we can say with confidence, "I shall rest and be filled; the Lord is Jehovah-Shalom" (see Judg. 6:24). He is God, our Peace. When our hunger and thirst have been satisfied and we are lying down in safety, then our hearts are at rest. We are at peace. The Lord, our Shepherd, gives us rest.

When we trust our Shepherd and follow Him, we can say, "I shall be led to places where my thirst is met; the Lord is the water of life." Jesus told the Samaritan woman at Jacob's well in Sychar, "Everyone who drinks this water will be thirsty again, but whoever drinks the water I give him will never thirst. Indeed, the water I give him will become in him a spring of water welling up to eternal life" (Jn. 4:13b-14). Sometime later in Jerusalem during the Feast of Tabernacles Jesus stood and proclaimed, "If anyone is thirsty, let him come to Me and drink. Whoever believes in Me, as the Scripture has said, streams of living water will flow from within him" (Jn. 7:37b-38). How can a sheep who is being taken care of so well ever want another shepherd?

The pastor models this trusting life as a sheep. As he is led by still waters, and as he lies down, rests in green pastures, and drinks from the water of life, he says to the congregation, "I don't want any shepherd but Jesus. I'm not going to serve or follow anyone else." His example shows his sheep what it means to follow Christ, so that by his example they too can learn to follow Christ.

The Office of the Pastor

In Transition—Walking Through the Valley

*Yea, though I walk through the valley of the shadow of death,
I will fear no evil: for Thou art with me; Thy rod and Thy
staff they comfort me* (Psalm 23:4 KJV).

This verse represents a transition in which the sheep of
verses 1-3 is becoming a shepherd. Were the sheep still only
a sheep, the wording most likely would be, "Yea, though I *be
led* through the valley...." The word "walk" translates the
Hebrew word *yalak*, which in this context means "to walk" in
the sense of "to carry away" or "to lead forth."[6] Perhaps one
way to look at this would be to say, "Yea, though I *lead the way*
through the valley of the shadow of death...." This sheep is
becoming a shepherd; he is beginning to talk like a shepherd. The best shepherds are always those who have been
good sheep. They are effective leaders because they have
first learned how to follow.

What is the death referred to in "the valley of the shadow of death"? As far as the pastor/shepherd is concerned, it
is death to self; not a death imposed by others, but one
taken up willingly. The shepherd lays down his life for the
sheep. Jesus is the prime example of this. He is the Great
Shepherd who walked through His own death and, unlike
all other men, came out on the other side. Shepherds must
be willing not only to walk into their own deaths but also by
the resurrection power of Jesus Christ to come out on the
other side because they are walking with Him and are living
in His presence and power.

Those who have already died have nothing to fear from
death. Once we have walked through the valley of the shadow of death, what is left to cause us fear? The Lord's pres-

---

6. Strong, *yalak*, (H#3212).

ence sustains us. We can say, "I will fear no evil: for Thou art with me." The Lord our Shepherd is with us "through the valley of the shadow of death"; therefore, we "will fear no evil."

The Lord gives not only His presence, but also His protection. "Thy rod and Thy staff they comfort me." The rod (Hebrew *shebet*) was a stout, club-like stick used for fighting. Specifically, the shepherd used it to drive away wolves and other predators that threatened the flock. The staff (Hebrew *mish'enah*) was a walking-stick that served also to draw straying sheep back into the fold. Isn't it a comfort to know that our Lord has a stick in His hand to drive the enemy away and a staff to guide us back to Him and to help us stay in the "narrow way"?

From Sheep to Shepherd

Thou preparest a table before me in the presence of mine enemies: Thou anointest my head with oil; my cup runneth over. Surely goodness and mercy shall follow me all the days of my life: and I will dwell in the house of the Lord for ever (Psalm 23:5-6 KJV).

These verses reveal that the process is now complete. The sheep has grown into a shepherd. "Thou preparest a table before me in the presence of mine enemies...." Sheep don't eat at the table. This is a shepherd's feast. "Thou anointest my head with oil; my cup runneth over...." Sheep don't carry cups, either. This is a shepherd speaking. "Surely goodness and mercy shall follow me all the days of my life: and I will dwell in the house of the Lord forever." Sheep don't live in the house. This is a shepherd enjoying the presence of his Lord and God.

The Office of the Pastor

With so much talk in the Church these days about being "in the river," it's important to understand the particular significance of the phrase, "goodness and mercy shall follow me all the days of my life." When we get "into the river," we begin flowing with the current of God's Spirit, and His goodness and mercy sustain us. Any time we start to fall back or we enter a dangerous current in the river, God's goodness and mercy are right there to guide us back. The current leads us deeper and deeper into the dwelling place of God, where we will live with Him forever.

Working Together in All Things

The office of the pastor is to work with the other offices of the five-fold ministry. Pastors are not to be in competition with other leaders. This would seem to be an obvious statement, so why point it out with particular reference to the office of pastor?

For one thing, pastors face challenges that the other offices don't face, at least not often. The very gifting and role of pastors put them in the position of getting closer to the people on an everyday basis than the other offices. This can make them more emotionally and psychologically vulnerable. It is this very closeness and vulnerability that lends to the high stress levels and burnout that were mentioned at the beginning of this chapter.

All the offices of the five-fold ministry must learn from the others. They must learn to appreciate each other and to recognize their mutual need for one another. By receiving those who walk in the other offices, all will be more effective in their respective callings. In the midst of all this, I believe that there are two dangers that pastors, in particular, must watch out for.

Guard Against Jealousy

Pastors can be very jealous and protective of their sheep. There-fore, they have to watch out for this jealousy toward other gifts that are loved and liked. In other words, if you care about your sheep, it's easy as a pastor to reach the point where you want your sheep to care only about you. With this kind of mind-set, the presence of another gifted and powerfully anointed person can be viewed as a threat.

A few years ago a successful pastor invited me to preach a revival at his church. From the moment he met me at the airport it was obvious to me that he was the "pastor's pastor." His gifting as a shepherd was so abundant that it was almost dripping off of him.

He was one of those individuals who never meets a stranger. By the time we got out of that busy airport, he must have greeted literally dozens of people. He was trying to pastor everybody: the skycap, the ticket agent, the taxi driver.

When he found out that I had brought a supply of my teaching tapes with me, he assured me that I needn't have bothered. "My people believe that I am the greatest preacher in the world," he said. "They never listen to anyone else." Here was a gifted, caring pastor who didn't want his sheep listening to someone else.

As it turned out, every one of my tapes was sold after the Sunday morning service in which I spoke. There were none left. When the pastor was informed of this, I watched as all the blood drained out of his face. He had believed that his people wanted to listen only to him.

It was a terrible week for the pastor. People jammed the building every night and wouldn't leave before 11 or 12 o'clock, and they took in the largest offering they had ever received. However, I knew in my heart that when the next

The Office of the Pastor

Sunday rolled around, this pastor was going to start trying to undo everything that God had done, because throughout the week I had watched him become more and more jealous by the moment. I think he was afraid that I wanted his church—which I didn't—and that his people would want me—which they didn't. They welcomed me and responded because I had something to offer them that they wanted. That pastor's position and influence were never in jeopardy, but he was still jealous.

Guard Against Judgmental Attitudes

Pastors also have to watch out for judgmental attitudes toward gifts that are powerful and different. Over the last few years one of the questions I have been asked most frequently is whether or not I believe that the "laughing revival" is of God. This refers to the ministry of men like Rodney Howard-Browne and others, and the "Toronto Blessing" and their off-shoots.

A few years ago I attended a Rodney Howard-Browne meeting and took the most "melancholy" member of my church with me. He was the straightest of straight arrows. I don't think I had ever seen him laugh. My thought was that if *he* was touched by the "laughing revival," then I would *know* that it was of God. To make a long story short, he was powerfully touched...and so was I. I came away absolutely convinced that God was at work and that the "laughing revival" was truly a work of the Holy Spirit.

A few weeks later I was in a restaurant where I met two pastors who were old friends of mine. They too had attended these meetings. I had seen them there, and we had spent some time talking about what was going on. They had witnessed the same things I had. Yet when I greeted them in the restaurant, I was quite surprised to discover that the meetings that had meant so much to me had left them much less impressed. In fact, they both told me that they had decided that the revival was not of God. They even went so far as to attribute the whole things to demons.

I could hardly believe it. For a long time, I couldn't figure it out. How could they have seen the same things that I had seen and conclude that it wasn't of God? Over the last several years the Lord has given me a better understanding. Pastors sometimes become very critical of people like Benny Hinn, or Kathryn Kuhlman of a generation ago—people with dynamic, powerful ministries—out of fear that their people will give all their money, time, and accolades to them. It is very easy to become judgmental when you feel threatened or jealous.

Those with the gifting, ministry, and office of pastoring have a vitally important calling. However, it is slow work that requires steady patience and commitment and that often lacks the "glamour" of some of the other types of ministry. It's easy to look at those other ministries and say that they are not of God when the reality may be simply that God is not working through you that way. The ministries are different and the needs are different, but as different as they are, all are necessary parts of Christ's overall work of building His Church. We all must be careful that we don't judge other people's ministries as being not of God simply because they are different from ours.

Praying for Our Pastors

At the beginning of this chapter I said that unless a pastor makes known a particular request or a specific need, many people do not know how or what to pray for him on a regular basis. It is vitally important that we learn to continually lift up our pastors in prayer because they are constantly on the

The Office of the Pastor

spiritual firing line. I would like to close this chapter by listing eight specific ways that we can pray for our pastors.

1. ***Pray that he will be delivered*** from the disobedient—those who peddle doubt, those who are in opposition—and from those who are wicked and unreasonable people (see Rom. 15:30-31; 2 Thess. 3:2).

2. ***Pray that his service will be acceptable*** to the saints (see Rom. 15:18-19).

3. ***Pray that he will come to you with joy*** and a merry heart and with Holy Ghost laughter, for these will bring strength (see Ps. 28:7-8; 32:10-11; Prov. 17:22).

4. ***Pray that he will be refreshed daily*** and not grow stale spiritually (see 2 Cor. 1:10-11).

5. ***Pray for his protection*** and that he will be delivered from a great death sentence (becoming totally discouraged and burned out) (see 2 Cor. 1:8-9).

6. ***Pray that he will have doors opened by God*** to speak the mystery of Christ and to train young men to follow in his footsteps, ministering around the world (see Col. 4:3).

7. ***Pray that the Word of God in his life will have "free course"*** and be glorified, flowing freely from him to his people (see 2 Thess. 3:1 KJV).

8. ***Pray that the people he pastors will minister to him*** and his family in love (see Rom. 15:32).

Chapter Seven

The Office of the Teacher

And these words, which I command thee this day, shall be in thine heart: And thou shalt teach them diligently unto thy children, and shalt talk of them when thou sittest in thine house, and when thou walkest by the way, and when thou liest down, and when thou risest up (Deuteronomy 6:6-7 KJV).

And the things you have heard me say in the presence of many witnesses entrust to reliable men who will also be qualified to teach others (2 Timothy 2:2).

Educators tell us that a third-grade reading level is the benchmark educational level for success in our society. What this means is that anyone who can read and comprehend at a third-grade level can function adequately in life. Essentially, anyone with a third-grade education should be able to deal with the bank, the IRS, the government, or their jobs. I don't know what that says about the standards and expectations in our society, but I do know that all across the country, young people are graduating from high school when they are almost functionally illiterate. Many of them cannot read well enough to fill out a job application. Something is terribly wrong.

Not long ago I heard a report that the state of California was trying to stop schoolteachers from moving children through the school system before they were ready. Any student who had not achieved a third-grade reading level by the end of the third-grade year was not to be advanced to the fourth grade. This would seem to be an obvious point, yet due to teacher workload, the number of students, parental expectations, and other demands, many school systems across the country feel tremendous pressure to advance students whether or not they are ready.

According to another news report, 46 percent of third-grade students in the state of Texas read at lower than a third-grade level. Yet teachers, because of their load and other pressures, continue to push these children on. As a result, these students and others like them all across the country spend the rest of their school years in a struggle to catch up. They suffer from poor grades, low self-esteem, and often, ridicule from their peers. Many of them drop out of school. In most cases these children are not dumb; they have simply been pushed to levels they are not ready for.

To a great extent the Church has developed the same mentality. Our pews are full of people who have no grasp of even the most basic teachings of biblical truth. Many churches are made up mostly of believers who are functionally illiterate in spiritual matters. Yet we continue to press on, pushing many of these people into positions and ministries that they are in no way ready for, assuming that somewhere along the way they will somehow pick up the knowledge they need and get up to speed.

Unfortunately, learning rarely happens this way. Students need sufficient time to learn, absorb, and apply their knowledge. More importantly, they need skilled, dedicated teachers who can instruct them in what they need to know and help them understand and apply it. As in our general society, there is a great need in the Church for gifted teachers.

Out With Ignorance!

The ministry of teaching is the only gift found in all three lists of spiritual gifts, ministries, and functions set forth in the New Testament, which should give some clue as to its importance. God has set teachers into the Body of Christ to ground believers in the Word of God, to get them deeply rooted and established in the Lord, and to help cure and purge ignorance.

One indication of the teaching gift is a strong desire to impart illumination, knowledge, and understanding to other believers. Another sign of this gift is a demonstrated ability to present both simple and complex spiritual truths in an understandable manner. Quite often, "intellectuals" display the ability to make simple truths difficult. (How well many of us remember "teachers" like that when we were in school!) A gifted teacher, on the other hand, is able to make difficult truths simple.

Believers who are not well-grounded in the Word of God and the basic truths of the faith are particularly susceptible to deception and error. Gifted teachers see their ministry as helping to remove ignorance from believers who might otherwise fall prey to the snares and attacks of the enemy.

Luke is an excellent example of a New Testament teacher. Both the Gospel that bears his name and the Book of Acts were written for the purpose of illumination, knowledge, and instruction. For example, consider Luke's opening words to his Gospel:

> *Many have undertaken to draw up an account of the things that have been fulfilled among us, just as they were handed down to us by those who from the first were eyewitnesses and servants of the word. Therefore, since I myself have carefully investigated everything from the beginning, it seemed good also to me to write an orderly account for you, most excellent Theophilus, so that you may know the certainty of the things you have been taught* (Luke 1:1-4).

Luke wanted Theophilus to have clear and certain knowledge, as well as confidence in what he had been taught, so Luke set down an "orderly account." In other words, Luke was explaining complex spiritual truths in simple, straightforward, and understandable terms.

The Book of Acts is the same way. Very early on Luke presents his "outline" for the book: "But you will receive power when the Holy Spirit comes on you; and you will be My witnesses in Jerusalem, and in all Judea and Samaria, and to the ends of the earth" (Acts 1:8). The rest of the book is a well-organized, orderly development of this outline: chapters 1-7, the Church in Jerusalem; chapters 8-12, the Church expanding into Judea and Samaria; chapters 13-28, the Church expanding to the ends of the earth.

Communication Is the Key

Effective teaching involves successful communication between the teacher and the student. Communication is accomplished when the student hears what the teacher intended him to hear and understands it the way the teacher intended him to understand it. This means that for

The Office of the Teacher

learning to take place, communication between teacher and student must occur at more than just a superficial level.

The best teaching and learning occur in an environment where teacher and student can build a relationship that goes beyond the mere transfer of basic facts and knowledge. Good teachers impart learning at several different levels. At the most basic level, teachers teach by *precept*; the student's learning is based on what the teacher *says*. This is basic impartation of facts and information. Secondly, a good teacher teaches by example; precepts are reinforced by who the teacher is in the eyes of the student. Effective teachers also teach by *conduct*; the student's learning increases as he watches what the teacher *does* on a consistent basis. Finally, the most effective teaching occurs when the teacher models in his or her life the principles being taught. Studies have revealed that only three percent of learning is verbal. Thirty-eight percent is transmitted through attitude, while a full 55 percent comes from watching others. Good teachers recognize that learning is "caught" more than it is taught.

Jesus' relationship with His disciples is probably the best illustration of this. The 12 apostles walked with Jesus, lived with Him, and spent time with Him day in and day out. They listened to His words, observed His conduct and behavior, and learned as He modeled for them the truths and principles He taught. Jesus' actions reinforced His words, and the disciples "caught" what Jesus wanted them to learn.

The most effective teachers are those who remain lifelong learners themselves. Teachers who stop growing in their own knowledge become stale. For those who have the ministry of teaching in the Church, this means being diligent, lifelong students of the Word of God. It means making personal application of Paul's instructions to Timothy: "Study to show thyself approved unto God, a workman that needeth not to be ashamed, rightly dividing the word of truth" (2 Tim. 2:15 KJV). It means building a sound theology through a clear understanding of the foundational truths of God's Word. It means building on the firm foundation laid by the apostles and the prophets. The standard against which all teaching in the Church must be judged is the infallible Word of God.

Rightly Dividing the Word of Truth

The office of teacher in the five-fold ministry has the responsibility of training believers to live not just on the *inspiration* of God's Word, but also on the *instruction* of God's Word. The most familiar passage of Scripture relating to the very nature of Scripture itself contains both of these elements. "All scripture is given by inspiration of God, and is profitable for doctrine, for reproof, for correction, for instruction in righteousness: That the man of God may be perfect, thoroughly furnished unto all good works" (2 Tim. 3:16-17 KJV). God Himself *inspired* the Bible, which *instructs* believers in the ways of God. The Word of God comes to us by inspiration, but we receive it by instruction.

All of us know what it is like to be inspired by the Word of God. We hear someone preach the Word with power and it lifts us up and makes us feel that we can take on the world for Christ. We need those times, however, we cannot live all the time on inspiration alone. Sometimes we have to live by instruction. Inspiration is wrapped up in our emotions while instruction engages our minds. We can't live by what we feel; we must live by what we know. What we *feel* can change with the wind, but what we *know* never changes.

Gifted teachers rightly divide the Word of truth by taking difficult Bible doctrines and making them clear, simple, and palatable. They take complex teachings and concepts and break them down so that we are able to consume them. This also involves tailoring the teaching to fit the age, maturity, and development level of the learners. Thus, a good teacher knows how to take the "meat" of the Word and turn it into "milk" for those who are still babes in Christ. At the same time, he knows when and how to challenge believers to move forward to deeper and higher levels.

The office of teacher also bears the responsibility of teaching the ministry gifts. This means training the young apostles, the young prophets, the young evangelists, and the young pastors in the ways that God ministers through them, and helping them understand how to function in their respective callings. This is part of God's overall design to mature believers, bring better balance to the Body of Christ, and fulfill the work of the ministry.

By word and example a gifted teacher demonstrates that integrity comes from *being* rather than simply *doing*. The call to apostleship is the call to *be* an apostle, not simply to *do* the work of an apostle. The mantle of the prophet is not something that you can simply put on and take off whenever you feel like it. Prophetic office means *being* a prophet, not just acting like one. The call of Christ is a call to all of us, and it is a call to *be* more than it is a call to *do*. *Doing* simply identifies certain actions and behavior; *being* defines who we really are inside.

So it is not a matter of what we do but of who we are. As believers we are children of God with Christ as our Master. The gift we have each received is *Christ Himself*, living in us and working through us; or as Paul described it, it is "Christ in you, the hope of glory" (Col. 1:27b).

Finish the Lesson!

Gifted teachers understand that teaching is never complete until the learner has learned what is being taught. Teaching requires patience because it is often necessary to repeat the lessons for as long as it takes for the students to give evidence that they understand. This evidence will reveal itself in changed attitudes, behavior, and practice on the part of the students. It is not enough simply to impart information. The goal of all good teaching is to *change behavior.*

There was once a pastor who preached the same sermon to his congregation several weeks in a row. After about the third or fourth time one of his deacons challenged him. "Why have you preached the same sermon all month? Let's move on to something else." The pastor replied, "We'll move on to another message just as soon as you start living *this* one!"

The problem in churches today is not a lack of sermons. On the contrary, we probably have more sermons than we can handle. The truth of the matter is that until we start living the last message, we're really not ready for another one. We have become overweight with the Word of God to the point where instead of being doers of the Word, we are merely tasters of the Word. We taste a little here and a little there; and if we like it, we come back for more. If we don't like it, we just wait for something else. We like the teachings that make us feel good or that talk about the presence of God, the blessings of God, and the power of God—things that give us "goose bumps." Less tasteful are those teachings that call on us to do something, to change something, or to make a sacrifice. We want to indulge our spiritual "sweet tooth" all the time while neglecting the "fruits and vegetables" that are the key to balanced and healthy growth.

The Office of the Teacher

I'm sure we have all seen the growing number of books written for "dummies": "Computers for Dummies," "Car Repair for Dummies," "Math for Dummies," etc. I think that someone should write one entitled "The Bible for Dummies" because there are so many people sitting in the pews of our churches who are biblically illiterate. The Church by and large has failed to provide these folks with adequate grounding in the fundamentals of the faith. Yet so often we expect them to move in the deeper things of God when they still don't understand the basics.

The office of the teacher has the responsibility to recognize that teaching is not complete until the learners have demonstrated by changed lives that they understand what they have been taught.

A Balanced Diet

Although the office of the teacher may function independently, it works best when used to complement the other offices of the five-fold ministry. This cooperation promotes a balanced spiritual diet in the Church. A biblical example of this is the church at Antioch.

In the church at Antioch there were prophets and teachers: Barnabas, Simeon called Niger, Lucius of Cyrene, Manaen (who had been brought up with Herod the tetrarch) and Saul. While they were worshiping the Lord and fasting, the Holy Spirit said, "Set apart for Me Barnabas and Saul for the work to which I have called them." So after they had fasted and prayed, they placed their hands on them and sent them off (Acts 13:1-3).

The church at Antioch had "prophets *and* teachers." These two offices really complement each other. Prophets receive and communicate revelation (Greek, *apokalupsis*)

131

and knowledge (Greek, *gnosis*), whereas teachers give instruction (Greek, *didaskalia*). Prophets speak the Word of the Lord to us, while teachers help us to understand what it means and how to apply it to our lives. With both prophets *and* teachers on hand in the fellowship, the church in Antioch had balance.

During a time of worship and fasting, the Holy Spirit set apart Paul and Barnabas for mission work to preach the gospel and plant churches. After more fasting and prayer, "they placed their hands on them and sent them off." Verse 4 says that Paul and Barnabas were sent on their way "by the Holy Spirit." The Spirit sent them out, but not until after the prophets *and* the teachers at Antioch had placed their hands on them.

Barnabas and Paul were apostles, yet they received the spirit of prophecy from the prophets and the spirit of understanding and instruction from the teachers. When they departed from Antioch, Paul and Barnabas therefore had the ability both to prophesy and to teach. The Spirit of God had imparted to Paul and Barnabas, through the prophets and teachers, the ministry gifts needed for apostleship.

The point of all this is that teachers, prophets, evangelists, pastors, and apostles are supposed to work together, not separately. One gift cannot do all the work of the ministry in the local church. We all need each other. The problem is that most of us grew up in a traditional church where one person was recognized as the pastor and leader of the church. The concept of different individuals working together with equal authority in equal but different ministries is still foreign to most of us.

What we need to remember is that Christ is building *His* Church and He is building it according to *His* pattern.

The Office of the Teacher

It was He who gave some to be apostles, some to be prophets, some to be evangelists, and some to be pastors and teachers, to prepare God's people for works of service, so that the body of Christ may be built up until we all reach unity in the faith and in the knowledge of the Son of God and become mature, attaining to the whole measure of the fullness of Christ. Then we will no longer be infants, tossed back and forth by the waves, and blown here and there by every wind of teaching and by the cunning and craftiness of men in their deceitful scheming. Instead, speaking the truth in love, we will in all things grow up into Him who is the Head, that is, Christ. From Him the whole body, joined and held together by every supporting ligament, grows and builds itself up in love, as each part does its work (Ephesians 4:11-16).

None of the ministry gifts are more or less important than any of the others; rather, all are needed. Each gift, each ministry, each office, each person must be in place working together in unity and harmony. Otherwise there will be an incomplete picture, an off-balance viewpoint, a stunted church, a withered hand. There must be balance.

A Local Presbytery

The teacher in office functions along with prophets and apostles as a local presbytery, which involves three main elements, all of which were operating in the church at Antioch:

1. The ministry of fasting. The prophets and teachers at Antioch were worshiping, fasting, and praying when the Holy Spirit spoke to them. I have often thought of fasting as a duty, but only recently in my life have I begun to understand it as a ministry. What I have come to realize is that when apostles, prophets, and teachers begin functioning and fasting together, then God begins to speak in mighty ways.

2. *Awareness of the direction and the directives of the Holy Spirit.* The leaders at Antioch heard the voice of the Spirit and understood what He was telling them to do. This awareness and sensitivity to the Spirit helps the local presbytery give guidance to the churches.

3. *Accountability to God for the ministry of the laying on of hands.* The prophets and teachers at Antioch laid hands on Paul and Barnabas, thus imparting to them through the power of the Spirit the gifts of prophecy and teaching. Because of the power of impartation, this is a serious and important responsibility. Teachers are involved in the laying on of hands because of the transfer of spirits.

An Alert Watchman

A teacher in office is a watchman for false teachers. The Old Testament contains repeated warnings against false prophets, and Ezekiel deals with false shepherds. The New Testament has much to say about the threat of false teachers. Since its earliest days the Church has had to guard against false teachers of every description. Jesus, Paul, Peter, and John all warned against the danger of false teachers coming in among the flock and deceiving and scattering the sheep. The danger is just as real today as it was then.

How do you tell the difference between a true teacher and a false one? Some false teachers are so shrewd, so subtle, and so clever that what they have to say sounds good, solid, and quite appealing. The simplest answer is that a true teacher *always* points to *Christ*, while a false teacher points to himself. A false teacher is always exalting his own message and agenda.

It is not in the sense that Paul meant when he said, "Therefore I urge you to imitate me" (1 Cor. 4:16), but rather in the sense of "Look at me and how great I am." Whenever the object of teaching becomes the teacher, then

The Office of the Teacher

the teaching is false and so is the teacher. True teachers don't point us to a denomination, a tradition, a ritual, or even a book; they point us to a Person, Jesus Christ. True teachers keep the focus of their teaching squarely on Christ so that He gets the glory. Jesus said, "But I, when I am lifted up from the earth, will draw all men to Myself" (Jn. 12:32). True teachers lift up Jesus so that men are drawn to Him. True teachers have the gift of discerning between true and false teaching and of distinguishing between the wolves and the true sheep. This is one reason why they are so important to the Church. A local church without true teachers is vulnerable to being misled and sidetracked. On the other hand, a church that calls out true teachers and recogizes their office provides a setting in which believers and seekers alike can be founded and established in the Word of God, thereby deepening their relationship with the Word Himself, the Lord Jesus Christ.

Chapter Eight

The Withered Hand Restored

We live in a society that is driven by the pursuit of wealth on the one hand and the pursuit of pleasure on the other hand. Americans have an almost obsessive desire for entertainment of any kind. It has become a multi-billion dollar industry. Television is one of the major forces behind our preoccupation with being entertained. It is so much easier to let our television think for us and do our entertaining for us than it is to challenge ourselves to higher pursuits.

Unfortunately, this "TV mentality" has made its way into the Church. We now have two generations who have been raised with television and who have learned to compartmentalize their minds into 30-second, 60-second, and 30-minute time segments. Attention spans have decreased while the expectation of excitement, thrill, and spectacle have increased. Many believers come to church expecting to be entertained. As far as they are concerned, that's what church is all about anyway. They have seen the ministry gifts in action through ministry programs on Christian television and have come to think of them as just another form of entertainment. Consequently, when they come to church they expect the apostle, the prophet, the evangelist, the pastor, and the teacher to entertain them. These entertainment-seeking church members are like the little boy who went to church, put 25 cents in the offering, and replied, when asked after the service how he liked it, "It was a pretty good show for a quarter."

The ministry gifts are not for entertaining the saints, but for equipping them to do the work of the ministry. Being equipped is rarely entertaining. Neither is the process of maturing. These experiences may engage our attention and perhaps even be exciting at times, but they are not entertaining. Instead, in a seeker-sensitive culture we must be careful to reproduce the servant qualities revealed to us in God's Word. The Church suffers from too many shallow decisions made by too many people who have too little understanding of what they are doing. It's one thing to motivate saints to mark their Bibles; it's quite another to motivate saints to allow the Holy Spirit to mark *them*. Too often people indicate that they have made a decision for Christ, but their attitude and behavior afterward make it hard to tell *what* decision they made! The purpose of the five-fold ministry is to prepare, mend, and shape-up the saints. This is done by encouraging Christians to seek spiritual gifts and by showing them how to function in the gifts for the edification of the Body of Christ.

Healthy Hand, Balanced Church

When the five-fold ministry is fully recognized, acknowledged, and allowed to function as the Lord intended when He gave these gifts, the result for the Church will be peace, harmony, and balance. No longer will there be a withered hand. All "fingers" will be whole, every gift will be recognized, and every part of the Body will be in place and operating according to their gifting.

It's important at this point to understand how the five-fold ministries operate together in their offices. They truly do complement each other, each one carrying out an important and specific function for the building and strengthening of the Church. The following breakdown into two columns will help illustrate the vital relationship that exists between these offices.

Inspirational	*Logical*
Preaching—Quickening	Teaching—Illuminating
Appeals more to emotion than logic.	Appeals more to intellect than emotion.
Evangelists *gather.*	Pastors *guard.*
Prophets *guide.*	Teachers *ground.*

Apostles govern.

The "Inspirational" column has to do with the heart and focuses on feelings, the emotional side of our being. The "Logical" column relates to the things of the mind and focuses on thinking, which involves the intellectual and mental side of our being.

Preaching is an inspirational activity. It quickens the heart and appeals more to the emotions than to logic. Teaching, on the other hand, is a logical activity that illuminates the mind and appeals more to the intellect than to emotion. Both sides are important for a balanced faith. Preaching puts the fire in our faith; teaching establishes our faith on a firm foundation. As Paul said to the Corinthians, "I will pray with the spirit, and I will pray with the understanding also: I will sing with the spirit, and I will sing with the understanding also" (1 Cor. 14:15b KJV).

On the inspirational side, evangelists gather. As we have seen, evangelists have a great passion for the souls of men. Their preaching appeals to the emotional side, to the hearts of men to awaken them to their need to receive Christ as their Savior. Balancing on the logical side, pastors *guard*. We need the illuminating force of the pastor to keep and preserve all those whom the evangelist gathers. If we gather without guarding, many of those gathered will fall away. If we guard without gathering, before long there will be no one to guard. It's no fun standing guard at a cemetery! Evangelists and pastors together provide balance.

Again, on the inspirational side, prophets *guide*. They help the Church recognize and move toward its destiny. As a balance to the prophet on the logical side, teachers *ground*. Just as the prophet's preaching appeals to the emotional side of believers, the teacher appeals to their minds. Just as their hearts are stirred by the passion of the prophet, so their minds are grounded in God's Word by the patient toil of the teacher. If we have prophets but no teachers, then we will have excitement without depth, and enthusiasm without understanding. We will be like a river that is a mile wide and an inch deep. On the other hand, teachers without prophets will lead to understanding without passion. We will have much knowledge but no motivation to do anything with it.

Finally, apostles *govern*. Notice that the apostle is in the middle, being neither fully inspirational nor fully logical. This is because he operates in both. The apostle has the unique ability through the gifting of God to function in any of the other areas—not all the time, but as the need or circumstance arises. He can preach like a prophet, win the lost like an evangelist, ground believers like a teacher, and shepherd the flock like a pastor—whatever is needed.

The Hand Restored

The time has come for the Church to stop ignoring its withered hand. It's time for us to acknowledge the five-fold ministry as one of the key elements of the process by which Christ is building His Church. Jesus Christ is the Lord and the Head of the Church. He is building the Church for *His* glory, not for ours. The purpose of the five-fold ministry— the eldership of apostles, prophets, evangelists, pastors, and teachers—is to lift up Jesus Christ as the standard for the world. We are to live not to ourselves but to Christ. The only way we can do this is to allow Him to live His life in and through us.

When we allow the Lord to have His way, we will see the five-fold ministry grow to full maturity and effectiveness in our midst. Then the Church will once again exhibit the faith and foundation, the power and passion, of the true New Testament Church. *All* the saints will be trained, equipped, and built up to do the work of the ministry. No longer will Kingdom work be confined to only a select few or a particular building. The gospel of Jesus Christ and ministry in His name will flow out into the workplace and the home, into the malls and the grocery stores, into the slums and the suburbs, into the coffeehouses and the country clubs, into the cities and the country, to all nations, races, and people groups.

Gifts From the Ascended Christ

"Lord, build Your Church. Restore the hand of ministry that has become withered through neglect, misunderstanding, and unbelief. Equip Your people for the work of the ministry so that we, Your Body, may be built up until we all reach unity in the faith and in our knowledge of You. Bring us to full maturity, to the whole measure of Your fullness so that learning to speak the truth in love, we can work with You to reach a lost and dying world. In Jesus' name, amen."

ABOUT ROBERT D. STONE

Robert D. Stone is an author, minister, and speaker. He and his wife have been involved in full time ministry since 1977. Robert's personal mission is to lead people to a higher dimension of spiritual development and maturity.

Robert continues to travel, teach and encourage others to realize their full potential in Christ Jesus. He desires to write articles, books, and study helps that will live beyond his lifetime as a legacy of his faith in his Lord and Savior, Jesus Christ.

Robert's prayer for you is that you enter, embrace and enjoy an exciting and intimate relationship with the Lord Jesus Christ by the Presence and power of the Holy Spirit. He hopes that you will be changed from faith to faith and glory to glory through the Altar of His Presence.

Robert has been married to the love of his life, Susan, for over forty years. Together they have three children —Talitha, Tanyka, and Tyler.

ABOUT HIS MINISTRY

For more information about his ministry or materials
you can contact Robert directly by sending an email to him at
robertstone@destinyreformationministries.org
or info@altarofhispresence.com.

Be sure and visit Robert's weekly blog at
altaredsite.wordpress.com.

You can also listen to his audio podcast at
altarofhispresence.podbean.com.

Also, visit these other websites—

www.bishoprobertstone.com.

www.destinyreformationministries.org.

www.thealtarofhispresence.com.

www.altarofhispresence.com.

FREE E-BOOKS?
YES, PLEASE!

Get **FREE** and deeply discounted **Christian books** for your **e-reader** delivered to your inbox **every week!**

IT'S SIMPLE!

VISIT lovetoreadclub.com

SUBSCRIBE by entering your email address

RECEIVE free and discounted e-book offers and inspiring articles delivered to your inbox every week!

Unsubscribe at any time.

SUBSCRIBE NOW!